NOTE TO READER

This publication contains the opinions and ideas of its authors. It further includes the authors' general recollections of the events surrounding the *Costa Concordia* disaster to the best of their knowledge. The authors understand and acknowledge that their recollections of the events may conflict with or be inconsistent with the recollections of other survivors and witnesses of the *Costa Concordia* disaster. This book is not intended to be the definitive account of what occurred, but rather is intended to be a personal reflection of events that transpired from the authors' own experience and perspective. This book also contains the authors' tips for travelers based upon the authors' own travel experiences. The authors are not travel experts and do not purport to be authorities in this or any other respect with regard to this publication. Any travel tips provided by the authors are for informational and entertainment purposes only. Before following any travel tips provided in this book, you should speak with a travel expert and use your common sense and judgment. The authors and publisher specifically disclaim all responsibility for, and are not liable for, any liability, loss, or risk, personal or otherwise, which is incurred as a consequence, directly or indirectly, of the use and application of any of the contents of this book.

S.O.S.

Spirit of Survival

ONE FAMILY'S CHILLING ACCOUNT
OF THE COSTA CONCORDIA DISASTER

Dean Ananias, Georgia Gonos Ananias,
Valerie Joy Ananias, Debbie Karen Ananias,
and Cynthia Kristin Ananias

This book is dedicated to anyone who has ever been involved in a tragedy or traumatic event that occurred at sea and to their family and friends who have suffered with them along the way. The purpose of writing this book is to honor those who suffered aboard the *Costa Concordia*, and specifically those who lost their lives.

Dayana Arlotti	Egon Hoer
William Arlotti	Mylene Litzler
Elisabeth Bauer	Giovanni Masia
Michael Blemand	Thomas Alberto Costilla Mendoza
Maria D'Introno	Jean-Pierre Micheaud
Sandor Feher	Margarethe Neth
Horst Galle	Russel Terence Rebello
Josef Norbert Ganz	Inge Schall
Christina Mathi Ganz	Margrit Schroeter
Giuseppe Girolamo	Francis Servel
Jeanne Gregoire	Erika Fani Soria-Molina
Pierre Gregoire	Siglinde Stumpf
Gabriele Grube	Maria Grazia Trecarichi
Guillermo Gual	Luisa Antonia Virzì
Barbara Heil	Brunhild Werp
Gerald Heil	Joseph Werp

ACKNOWLEDGEMENTS

We wish to acknowledge all our family, friends, and colleagues that have shown us understanding, compassion, and expressed their love during this difficult time. For those of you that still remember what we have gone through, and you constantly help us get through each day, we will be forever grateful. To our dear Aunt Bessie Gonos, thank you for your unwavering support each and every day. You are a nurse by trade and our savior throughout this ordeal.

To Jonathan, the newest member of our family, we honor you and thank you for your help during this difficult time. We appreciate you more than you may ever realize.

To all the consummate professionals, our counselors and doctors, thanks for sharing your expertise and helping us through the many stages of trauma. We couldn't have done this book without your help and support.

We would like to express our deepest gratitude to all the wonderful people at Bird Street Books who provided guidance and enthusiastic encouragement during all the phases of this writing project.

To Scott Waterbury, thanks for making us feel like part of the Bird Street family. During our initial meeting, your kindness, empathy, and caring comforted us and encouraged us to write our story. You believed that our story needed to be told and you made it happen for us while taking into consideration how difficult this writing journey might be for all of us. You gave us your word that everyone would be sensitive to our needs and you stayed true to your word. We will be forever grateful and you will always be remembered fondly for your leadership, compassion, and enthusiasm.

Our grateful thanks are extended to Lisa Clark. We credit her with having the excellent vision to have this story told from five different voices. What an inspirational idea! Thanks so much for your help throughout this process. We couldn't have done this without you.

Special recognition goes to Rebecca Croes who knows our story better than anyone and who worked hard to assist all of us in every possible way! Her attention to detail added so much to making our story accurate and complete. She will be remembered for her hard work and dedication to our story.

To Jay McGraw, thank you for giving us this forum to tell people exactly what happened on the *Costa Concordia*. It is obvious that you have shown great leadership and monitored the process of this book personally and we appreciate that so much.

We must thank Dr. Phil and Robin for asking us to tell our story right after we returned from the disaster on the ship. We wanted to be able to tell about the events of that night in a safe place where people would be sensitive to us. They were very caring and helped us share our story with the world.

We would like to acknowledge all the other people that were on the *Costa Concordia* the night of the disaster. Though we all suffered anguish and grief, each of us experienced something different, and 32 people paid the ultimate price by losing their lives. We will always remember those that perished, as well as those that have had to learn to live with the consequences of that disastrous night. May all of you find some sense of peace in all of this as you move through the years.

We appreciate all the prayers we have received from around the world. Most of all, we thank God for guiding us during those lonely, frightful hours and for so many miracles and blessings along the way.

CONTENTS

PART TWO: SURVIVING ON SHORE

PART THREE: HOW YOU CAN SURVIVE

INTRODUCTION

In those first days after the accident, we were frequently asked what it was like being on the *Costa Concordia*. In an effort to help people understand what we had been through, Valerie related it to the movie *Titanic*. Her analogy drew some criticism in the weeks and months that followed. Then people began to realize that if not for a favorable wind, the death toll of the *Costa Concordia* could have been greater than that of the *Titanic*. We became curious about the aftermath of the *Titanic*'s ill-fated maiden voyage in 1912. What we found gave us hope that positive change could come as a result of our experiences, almost one hundred years later.

On April 15, 1912, the *Titanic* and more than fifteen hundred people went to the bottom of the North Atlantic. The circumstances surrounding the sinking sparked an immediate Senate investigation as well as a public outcry and media frenzy. People demanded answers. And they demanded change.

But even before *Titanic* set sail on her maiden voyage, she was already creating some negative stir, specifically regarding her size and her overly luxurious accommodations. *Titanic* weighed in around forty-six thousand tons, over a thousand more than her sister ship, the *Olympic*, and she stretched almost nine hundred feet from bow to stern, the equivalent of three football fields placed end-to-end. She was the largest ship of her time. But many distrusted the movement toward these floating monstrosities. Writer Joseph Conrad didn't believe that creating bigger ships was progress, stating, "If it were, elephantitis, which causes a man's legs to become as large as tree trunks, would be a sort of progress, whereas it is nothing but a disease, and a very ugly disease at that."

It wasn't just her size that people mistrusted. Among her other nicknames, *Titanic* was referred to as "the Millionaire's Special" and "the Last Word in Luxury." Had the industry become so caught up in making ships more and more luxurious to attract the world's richest passengers that it was sacrificing safety? The answer seemed clear following news of *Titanic*'s fate. Admiral Dewey, the man behind the victory at Manila Bay during the Spanish-American War, heard of the sinking and said,

> For myself, I would rather go around the world in a well-equipped man-of-war than make a trip across the North Atlantic in a transatlantic vessel. The greed for money-making is so great that it is with the sincerest regret that I observe that human lives are never taken into consideration.

Some of today's cruise liners would make the *Titanic* seem almost puny. The *Costa Concordia* held close to twice as many passengers and crew and weighed over twice as much as the *Titanic*. The cruising industry has also changed from a necessity, as it was before transatlantic flights were available, to a popular vacation choice for people all over the world. Yet these ships are still run by human beings, owned by corporations whose business it is to make money, and subject to the whims of Mother Nature. And sadly, despite all the changes that were made in light of *Titanic*'s demise, the recent rash of cruising "mishaps" in the past several years seems to indicate that many more changes are needed.

Within days of the *Titanic* disaster, Senator William Alden Smith of Michigan had formed an investigative Senate subcommittee to immediately question the surviving crew and passengers of the ill-fated ship. His mission was to determine what had gone wrong, what could be done to prevent another tragedy in the future, and to ensure that a treaty incorporating those preventative measures was drafted and signed into effect. Long before the Senate subcommittee issued any findings, some members of the press had already found the White Star Line (which owned the *Titanic*) and its parent company, the International Mercantile Marine (IMM), guilty of manslaughter and even murder. The *Philadelphia North American* went so far as to print an article entitled "Murder" and charged that

> the price was paid that will ever be paid until the will of nations forbids special privilege from using the bodies of men and women as counters in its private profit game. For that and no other is the silent message that seems to us comes from those men and women who lie murdered in the ocean depths.

The press, the Senate, and most importantly, the populace wanted answers to the many questions that had surfaced in the few days following the disaster. Why had Bruce Ismay, the president of IMM, managed to find himself among the seven hundred survivors when so many innocent people had not? Why were some survivors claiming that no warning bell had been rung alerting them to the danger? Why was the ship going so fast in an area known for its icebergs, and why wasn't the captain on the bridge for this dangerous part of the journey? Why had deck space designated for lifeboats been scrapped to make room for more first-class accommodations? Why was a higher percentage of the crew saved than either second- or third-class passengers? Why were there so few bodies found floating in their life jackets, and did it mean that there hadn't been enough life jackets, or worse, that hundreds of people had been trapped in the ship when it went down? And the questions just kept coming.

To answer those questions, Senator Smith and several others arrived in New York City in time to meet the *Carpathia* and the *Titanic* survivors she was carrying. Smith's goal was to prevent Ismay and certain members of the crew from returning to England in an effort to avoid facing a very unhappy United States. He achieved that goal and by 9:00 a.m. on Friday, April 19, just four days after the *Titanic* disappeared into the cold Atlantic waters, a reception hall at the Waldorf Astoria was standing room only and the questioning of Bruce Ismay and *Titanic*'s Second Officer Charles Lightoller was about to begin.

It would cover twelve days and two cities, but by the end of the investigation, Senator Smith would be very sure of one startling fact regarding the greatest maritime tragedy of all time: despite all the mistakes and all the bad decisions made by the corporation, the officers, and the crew, no one had technically done anything wrong—at least not according to current maritime law. And that bothered the senator very much.

In response to the tragic loss of Americans aboard the *Bourgogne* in 1896, the United States had passed the Harter Act, which gave passengers or their surviving family members the right to sue the company that owned the ship, so long as there was evidence that the company had knowledge of negligence on board. It was therefore of paramount importance that Senator Smith uncover some negligence that Bruce Ismay (as representative of IMM) had known about, in order for hundreds of affected Americans to have any legal redress for the tragedy.

Smith uncovered countless bad decisions and errors during the investigation, all of them perfectly legal. The *Titanic* was only carrying enough lifeboats to hold barely more than half of the passengers and crew. But that was sufficient for her to obtain her passenger certificate. In fact, *Titanic* had several *more* lifeboats than were legally required at the time. Unfortunately, as the ship was sinking, the crew was paranoid that the lifeboats, which were supposed to hold around sixty-five people, would buckle while being lowered if they were filled to capacity, so they under-filled most of them by at least half. The builders had specifically tested them to make sure that they would *not* buckle at maximum capacity—but no one thought to tell the crew about those tests.

And even if they had, the crew was sadly ill-prepared in regard to loading and lowering the boats because only one boat drill had been done and it had only involved two of the boats. The captain had canceled the boat drill scheduled for Sunday, April 14, for reasons unknown, leaving the crew altogether unprepared for the tragedy that would occur a mere twelve hours later—a fact eerily familiar to circumstances in another cruising disaster almost one hundred years after the *Titanic*. Unfortunately, the only legal requirement in 1912 regarding boat drills was that they be recorded in the ship's log, assuming they were even done at all.

The surviving crew member who had first spotted the iceberg while in the crow's nest stated that he and the other lookouts had requested binoculars but were denied them by the officers. When the senator inquired of others in the shipping industry as to whether binoculars were standard in the lookout perch (making it negligent to not have them), no one could agree. There was the same inconsistency when it came to testing the temperature of the water, by lowering a bucket over the side, in an effort to gauge the likelihood of ice in the vicinity. One passenger reported seeing a crew member fake the test using tap water from the boat because the rope wasn't long enough to get the bucket to the water. Apparently, faking the test wasn't negligence either because the shipping community couldn't agree on whether or not the test was even useful.

When it came to the collision with the iceberg, Senator Smith found more incompetence. The governing literature of the time specifically told how to maneuver a ship to avoid collisions such as this and urged against following the impulse to turn away and reverse the engines. And yet that was exactly what First Officer Murdoch had done in an attempt to avoid the iceberg—turned away and reversed the engines. Actually, had the ship just rammed headfirst into the berg, she probably would have been able to limp back to port, a conclusion supported by the same literature, which stated it was better for a ship to "present her stern to the danger rather than her broadside." As an experienced officer, Murdoch should have been familiar with the recommendations of the most prominent seamanship text; yet he went against it at every turn.

There was also sufficient evidence to suggest that while Captain Smith and Ismay had been blatantly aware of how dire the situation was within minutes of the collision, that fact was apparently not made obvious to the crew, who never displayed any sense of urgency when it came to evacuating the ship. But again, this breakdown in the chain of command couldn't be considered negligence on Ismay's part, especially since Ismay himself had spent most of his time on the sinking ship trying to help the crew get as many people as possible into the lifeboats.

Of major concern to the senator was the lack of regulation when it came to the wireless, the main form of communication aboard the *Titanic*. For starters, the wireless operators of the time were treated pitiably by the company that employed them. They worked long hours at a job fraught with pressure and were paid a whopping twenty dollars a month for their trouble. In addition to having no regulation of its workers, the wireless industry also enjoyed a lack of regulation regarding its communication traffic. Because of this, there was nothing to stop frivolous commercial messages (such as the ones being sent to and from the *Titanic* in the hours leading up to the collision) from taking precedence over warnings from other ships of the danger that lay ahead.

Time and time again, Senator Smith found himself bothered by the nonchalant attitude of most of the testifying expert seamen in regard to the utter lack of regulation and consistency surrounding the shipping industry. Smith was very familiar with the extensive laws governing the railroads, having worked on some of the legislation himself. It was appalling to him that the same basic industry that existed on the seas was much less regulated than its counterpart on land. Something needed to be done before more lives were lost.

So on May 28, 1912, after an extensive and emotional speech to a packed Senate chamber, Smith introduced Senate Bill Number 6976, which eventually became known as the Smith Bill. The bill addressed everything from the types of bulkheads on future passenger ships to the number of lifesaving devices and the types of lifeboats allowable. It also contained a complete overhaul of regulations governing the wireless. While not all parts of the bill passed, it did dramatically change the rules governing transoceanic travel. Furthermore, the Senate had already passed the Smith-Martine Resolution, which called for an international agreement regarding safe traveling on the seas. This resolution resulted in an international conference and the first version of the International Convention on the Safety of Life at Sea (SOLAS). To this day, SOLAS remains the governing document for maritime safety. A later bill—the Seamen's Act of 1915—would be presented and eventually passed, calling for the better treatment and training of seamen.

Overall, thanks to Senator Smith and other motivated politicians, the disaster of the *Titanic* would not be in vain, and traveling by sea would be forever safer than it had previously been. But a hundred years have gone by since the majority of that action was taken, and while sea travel is no longer a necessity in getting from one continent to another, millions of people now see cruising as a convenient and enjoyable means of vacationing. And yet they have significantly fewer rights on a cruise ship than they might suspect—thanks in part to ticket-purchase contracts and the all-important bottom line of most cruising corporations.

The death toll of the *Costa Concordia* disaster could have easily been as high or higher as that of the *Titanic* but for a favorable wind that blew the ship back up against the rocks and prevented it from sinking in deep water. Almost twice as many people were cruising or employed on that ship, compared to the *Titanic*, and there is no way to know how many of them would have lost their lives if the wind had been blowing out to sea instead of in towards land. As it is, thirty-two people are either dead or missing, and very little has been done to prevent this tragedy from happening again.

Since then, several more cruising catastrophes have occurred, thankfully with minimal loss of life, but it is clear from the increasing number of issues on cruise ships that something needs to be done. Action must be taken to ensure that cruise lines have the safety of passengers as their primary concern, rather than focusing on profit at the expense of passenger welfare. It is time for another Senator Smith to step up and be the voice of those who have suffered or died while at the mercy of the cruising industry.

In the meantime, it's important that people understand the legal and personal risks they take when cruising. Until the cruising corporations are forced to change, either by stricter regulations or public demand, it's unlikely that they will. So knowledge and preparedness are the keys to safe cruising. Just being aware of the dangers that can occur on a cruise ship and the limited rights that you have as a passenger is at least a safeguard against becoming another cruise ship casualty, either physically or financially.

Up until our experience on the *Costa Concordia*, our family loved cruising, and it was truly a part of our family's dynamic—a part that we still miss a year and a half later. We can only hope that telling our story can inspire change so that others won't ever have to go through a similar experience. Our motivation to write this book is to advocate for safety changes in the cruising industry. We hope that people can learn enough from our experience to protect themselves as much as possible until positive changes are made.

This book is written from all five of our voices. Four of us were on the ship—Georgia, Dean, Valerie, and Cindy. Debbie was back in the States, praying for the safety of the rest of us and working to get us home. Each of us on the ship had a similar experience, but we all came from unique personal perspectives and feelings, so sometimes we will tell you the same part of the story, but through two or three different points of view. Through it all, we have remained a strong family who continues to recover from our experiences on the *Costa Concordia*—and we are now dedicated to helping others, both by advocating for change and by sharing some vital need-to-know information with you before you take your next vacation.

PART ONE:

SURVIVING THE SHIPWRECK

CHAPTER:

PROLOGUE

NAME:

GEORGIA

DATE:

1/7/12 – 1/11/12

On Saturday, January 7, 2012, we were happily celebrating the wedding of our daughter Debbie and her fiancé Jonathan and their take on a traditional Greek wedding. Looking back, I'm painfully aware that it was almost our last big family celebration.

Debbie and Jonathan's engagement was a fairly short four months, due to Jonathan's demanding school schedule. Needless to say, the busy months leading up to the wedding were extremely exciting and filled with numerous events. So on top of throwing an engagement party and planning for a wedding, we also decided to plan a getaway vacation for after the celebrations were over. It had been years since we had been to Greece as a family, and the girls wanted to go back and experience it as adults. Luckily, our other daughters Valerie and Cindy both had a little free time in their schedules, which was not likely to happen again for quite some time. As avid cruisers, it only seemed logical that we find a cruise that would allow us to explore Greece and the Mediterranean. Eventually, we booked two back-to-back cruises that would cover everything from Greece to the Holy Land. The first of these was through Costa Cruises, which is owned by the Carnival Corporation.

My husband Dean and I had probably been on at least sixty cruises by that point in our lives. Our daughters had been with us for many of those trips and we had come to see cruising as a great way to make memories together as a family. In fact, my parents, Bessie and Jim, had started this family tradition by taking us all on cruises when the girls were very young. Up until January of 2012, it was a tradition we all loved and cherished. My "happy place" was always on a ship, cruising through the glistening water and visiting fascinating places. But it's amazing how quickly something special and meaningful can turn into something entirely different.

We told very few people about our plans because we didn't want to take away from Debbie and Jonathan's big day. Debbie knew, of course. (We all agreed it was going to be really strange and a little sad traveling without her since we were so used to all going together. We justified her not being with us because we knew she had planned a fantastic honeymoon cruise to Europe and that we would take many more cruises together with her and her new husband in the years to come.) We also told my cousin and my Aunt Bessie, or "Aunt B" as the girls call her, and a few other close family and friends. Other than that, no one knew of our post-wedding trip. Our focus and attention was to be on Debbie and Jonathan's wedding day!

The day of the wedding turned out almost as perfectly as we had hoped. It was very important to Debbie to have her grand-mother present at her wedding. My mom has fairly advanced dementia, but we knew her wish would be to take part in her granddaughter's important day. We had planned to bring her to the wedding so that she could at least walk in with me during the family processional. Once the wedding started, the plan was to have her caregiver take her back out because it would be too stressful for her to be around people she once knew but couldn't converse with anymore. There wasn't a dry eye in the church as my mom and I walked down the aisle of the beautiful cathedral. Surprisingly though, when we asked if she was ready to go, she stated with perfect clarity, "I can't leave; this is my family and I have to be here with them." Of course, at that point, we let her stay and she intently listened to the service and seemed to really enjoy the ceremony. I'm sure on some level she knew this was a very special day in the lives of her family members and that made her overjoyed. This was more than I could have hoped for, and it provided all of us with a lasting memory, which we will always treasure.

I say it turned out almost as perfectly as we had hoped because, well, no wedding is complete without someone forgetting something. In Debbie's wedding, it was the rings. Instead of the rings being brought into the church, they were left in the car! When the priest realized the rings weren't there, he gave the best man two minutes to retrieve them. The best man turned and bolted down the side of the church, out the doors, and through the parking lot to the car to grab the rings. Within a minute or so, he was back in the church making his way to the front again, much to the bewilderment of the guests, who had no idea that the rings were missing. Everyone at the altar knew what had happened, but Debbie and Dean had no idea what was going on! Luckily, after that, everything was smooth sailing.

For Dean, Debbie was the first of his daughters that he would walk down the aisle, and as he later realized, she was almost the last. This would become a genuine reality check for Dean as to just how much we almost lost. But on that day, he was thrilled to be walking down the aisle with his beautiful daughter. As they were waiting their turn to come down, Debbie kept looking at the watch Dean was wearing. When he noticed her glances, he told her that, in honor of the day, he had decided to wear my dad's watch, which my mom had given to Dean after my dad passed away. The watch stood in for my brother as well, who had also passed on. Dean wanted to wear it so that Debbie would know that her grandfather and her dear Uncle Jimmy were there with us in spirit on her wedding day. So not only did my mom get to participate, but we felt like we had my dad and brother with us as well. For a family as close as we are, things like that are incredibly important.

Overall, our family remembers Debbie's wedding as one of the best days of our lives. It was beautiful and it was fun. We all love Jonathan and were so happy to officially welcome him into the family. Cindy and Valerie got to stand up with Debbie, who is not just a sister, but also a best friend to them. And Dean and I enjoyed watching our family come together to celebrate such an amazing couple. It's surreal to look back now and see how different things would be just one week later.

The Monday following the wedding, Jonathan had to return to the University of Southern California, so the plan was for them to take their honeymoon cruise in May. But long before the wedding date had been set, Debbie had committed to spending a few days in Miami with some friends on that second week in January. Jonathan told Debbie she needed to go ahead with her plans since he would be busy with his engineering courses, and the short trip had been planned long before their engagement. So within days of the wedding, Debbie was preparing to head east to see some friends, Jonathan was starting a new semester, and the rest of us were gearing up for a one-month vacation overseas.

Since this was such a long trip, I decided to sit down with Debbie before she left and go over some legal matters with her, just in case something happened to us. Normally, I just sit down with our attorney before we leave to make sure things are in order, but this time I decided it might be good to go over some important family information with her as well. Mainly, I wanted to discuss how my mom should be provided for, what important financial information Debbie needed to know, and how we wanted our business to operate while were gone and in the event that we didn't return. It was a very in-depth conversation and it wound up being a little difficult for Debbie, but I felt better knowing she would be prepared, just in case. Oddly enough, despite all the cruises we had been on, I had never once sat down with a family member to go over how we wanted matters handled if we didn't return. Maybe it was the length of the trip or the recent wedding, but for whatever reason, this time it seemed important to me to have that difficult conversation.

Debbie had already had such major changes take place in her life in the last few days that—seeing the additional emotional toll the discussion was starting to take on her—I decided to lighten the mood a little. So I reminded her that if I didn't make it back, she'd have to be in charge of a large wedding shower I was planning. Since every woman knows how much time and preparation are involved in throwing showers, maybe my not coming back wasn't such a bad idea after all! She looked panicked and we both laughed and after that everything seemed all right again. But the night before Debbie's flight, she came back by the house to say good-bye and, as she was leaving, very unexpectedly burst into tears and told us she didn't want us to go! Dean and I were shocked because of how uncharacteristic it was of Debbie to be so affected like that. Worse, she couldn't even articulate why she was upset about it and was almost as confused by her feelings as we were.

We consoled her as much as we could without knowing what was bothering her about us leaving and she eventually returned home to finish getting ready for her trip. Dean and I attributed it to all the emotions that went along with the wedding. By the next morning, Debbie was heading to Miami for a few days and we were finishing up last minute details before our Thursday morning flight. Never did I envision or suspect that we were headed for a disaster at sea that would forever change our lives and the lives of more than four thousand people aboard the *Costa Concordia*. All of us would soon gather on board the ship with one goal in mind—the perfect cruising vacation.

CHAPTER:

ONE

NAME:

CINDY

DATE:

1/12/12

On Thursday morning, we were at the airport and ready to start the first leg of our journey, which took us to Atlanta. I was incredibly excited about this trip, and it had been all I could think about since it was planned. I had been to Italy and Greece before, but only as a little girl. I couldn't wait to go back as an adult and explore the Mediterranean. The fact that we were also going to Israel made it even more amazing.

The only thing that made this trip a little weird for me was that Debbie was left out. Normally we either travel together as a family, or my sisters and I go together, or we go individually with friends. But never does our family go as a group and leave one person out. My sisters and I are very close and while I was thrilled to get to spend the trip with Valerie, we were both pretty bummed that Debbie wouldn't be with us. It gave the trip a kind of bittersweet feel to it.

We travel as a family a lot, so waiting on a flight together is pretty much no big deal for everyone—except me. I'm afraid of flying. Now I understand that most people who are afraid

I'VE NEVER BEEN AFRAID TO BE ON A SHIP.
I LOVE THE WATER AND I LOVE BEING UP
ON THE HIGHEST DECKS OF THE SHIPS AND
LOOKING OUT AT EVERYTHING AROUND ME.

of flying just don't fly much, but that's not the case with me. I actually fly quite frequently. Usually the night before I fly, I get really nervous and my thoughts start to race about all that could go wrong. My stomach is tied in knots on the way to the airport. (Oddly enough, my nervousness about flying is usually mixed with an excitement to be going somewhere and traveling.) Most of the time, I take something to help my nerves before take-off. It never completely alleviates the anxiety, but it's better than nothing. Take-off is when I'm the most scared. The descent and landing doesn't really bother me.

To help cope with taking off, I generally put in earplugs and pray really hard and hold on tight to the arms of the seat. As long as it's a smooth ascent, I can make myself breathe through it and be okay the rest of the flight. But if there's any kind of turbulence or bumpiness at the beginning, I get very scared and start to panic. To help, when I fly with my family, I try to sit in between two of them and keep my head down—although recently I've been making myself look out the window, to help alleviate the anxiety.

Ironically, I've never been afraid to be on a ship. I love the water, and I love being up on the highest decks of the ships and looking out at everything around me. For some reason, I feel completely grounded on a ship. Something about a ship and the movement of the waves just makes me feel very calm. The rougher the seas, the more I enjoy it—pretty much the opposite of how I am in the air.

It's not that I've never had cause to worry on a ship—as a cruising family, we've had a few nerve-wracking moments. One time, I was sharing a room with my aunt and we were in our cabin sleeping when we were literally thrown off our beds by a sudden lurch. The tilt was bad enough that we basically had to crawl up to the door, but once the ship righted itself, we quickly forgot about it. It definitely wasn't anything that made me nervous to cruise again.

Our time at LAX that morning wasn't entirely worry free. My dad has high blood pressure and before we left California, Mom had checked it to see if it was in the normal range. Unfortunately, it was fairly high. She didn't tell my dad what it was, but she did let Valerie and I know that she was concerned about it and that worried us too. I guess you could say it changed my focus from being nervous about the flight to being worried about Dad. I remember Mom saying we would go ahead and fly to Atlanta and take his blood pressure again there to see if it was closer to normal. If it wasn't, she wanted Valerie and me to fly on ahead to Rome while she got Dad to a doctor and then they would catch up to us. Val and I immediately shot this down because we didn't want to split up from them. Either we all went together or we all stayed together.

Mom called Debbie from the airport to let her know about Dad's blood pressure and our plans. When we got to Atlanta, my mom checked his blood pressure and found it still hadn't gone down. We didn't have much time in Atlanta, thanks to a change in our terminal and a crazy dash from one end of the airport to the other, so we had to decide right away. Mom called Debbie back to tell her it was still high but that we were going ahead with the trip. She thought that telling Dad we weren't going might do him more harm than just getting on the plane, since she'd kind of kept him in the dark about how high his blood pressure was and he didn't have a headache or any other symptoms to make us worry more. Mom had some extra medicine for him, so she decided to give it to him and hope he could sleep on the plane. Debbie asked us to let her know how Dad was when we got to Rome, and Mom said we would. By the time we landed the next morning, Dad was fine and we were in Rome!

CHAPTER:

TWO

NAME:

VALERIE

DATE:

1/13/12, 8:00AM–9:30PM CET

It was Friday the thirteenth, but none of us gave it any thought at the time, not even me. Usually I notice, since thirteen is my favorite number and my birth date, but I guess I was too busy being thrilled that this trip was finally underway. For months, this had been so much more than just a vacation to me. It was a journey back to my roots, the place my family had originally come from. Going to Greece as an adult was about reconnecting with a part of me I didn't even know yet. It was about exploring the culture of the Mediterranean—the art, the history, the cuisine! It was about the voyage from there to the Holy Land, a place I had wanted to go my entire life. To be able to visit all of these amazing places on one trip, and get to take not one but two cruises, was almost more than I could fathom.

I had so many hopes and dreams wrapped up in this trip. I was still on an emotional high after Debbie's wedding and I had always felt a need to visit the Holy Land and Greece—I could feel an almost spiritual tug that had been drawing me to that area for so long. Being at the beginning of such an extraordinary

FOR MONTHS, THIS HAD BEEN SO MUCH MORE
THAN JUST A VACATION TO ME. IT WAS A
JOURNEY BACK TO MY ROOTS, THE PLACE MY
FAMILY HAD ORIGINALLY COME FROM.

and long-desired journey was incredible for me. I really felt like
I *needed* to make this trip at this point in my life. The thought of
being able to travel with my family, even though I missed Debbie,
made it more phenomenal. It was a huge priority on my bucket
list, and here I was, hours away from its onset.

And then it all went sideways.

Within a few hours of landing in Rome, things started to seem
"off" with this cruise. My dad had arranged for a nice shuttle to
take us to the port in Civitavecchia where we would meet up with
the *Costa Concordia*, the first of our two cruise ships. Our driver
was Romanian and he told us how beautiful he had heard the
ship was. I was getting more and more excited with every passing
mile and loved watching the scenery as we drove.

We got to the port around ten in the morning. We knew we
would have to wait a while to board because the passengers were
still disembarking from the previous cruise. Normally, cruise
lines are very organized at the port and have signs up telling the
passengers where to take their luggage, where to check in, and
where to get any other information. Apparently, that was not the
case with this cruise. There was security, but otherwise it was very
disorganized. The Costa representatives were chatting with each
other, busy with their cell phones, playing on the computers, and

just generally not engaged with the passengers. There didn't seem to be a desire to make a good first impression on the passengers. I doubt that was the employees' fault—it was probably a lack of training and supervision by the corporation. Still, it was frustrating.

We finally asked one representative where we needed to drop off our luggage and were sent over to one area of the docks. But from that point, another representative sent us to a different area, so we wound up dragging our baggage around for a while before we finally figured out where it was supposed to go. I would almost say the situation was one of mild chaos, in contrast to the normal organization at ports that we had experienced on our other cruises. The representatives weren't especially friendly and they didn't seem eager to welcome us. Most of the time passengers are treated really well prior to boarding because cruise lines want to make a good first impression. They usually have refreshments available and generally try to create a welcoming atmosphere. Unfortunately that wasn't the case here.

I was getting more and more frustrated with the situation, so while my mom, dad, and sister sat and rested, I told them I was going to try to find out what was going on from some of the Costa representatives. Normally I'm not the assertive one in the family, but I tend to step up more at times like this, maybe because I dislike disorganization so much. I found a representative and asked what time we were going to be able to board and whether she needed my credit card yet—just general questions that usually would have been answered before I even had to ask. I was trying to convince myself that the difference in procedure was because we were in Europe where things are a little more laid back. But instead of answering any of my questions, the representative told me not to worry about it and to take a seat and they would call us when things were ready. I didn't get a single specific answer.

Walking back to my family, I struck up a conversation with another American who mentioned that he was also frustrated and fed up with the lack of organization. He had cruised with the company before and said that, while they were never as organized as other lines, they had never been *this* disorganized before. He had been trying to get information regarding his wife, who was in a wheelchair, and he hadn't been able to get any useful instructions from the representatives. I could tell he was fairly annoyed about it and I didn't blame him for feeling that way.

I headed back over to where my family was waiting and Mom, Cindy, and I decided to go explore the town rather than sit around at the port indefinitely. Civitavecchia is known to be a pretty quaint little Italian village with a lot of cute shops on its main street. We certainly didn't have anything else to do while we waited for the cruise representatives to finally get organized. Plus, Mom thought she could use an additional coat since the weather was colder than we had expected it to be. So we wandered into town and checked out a few of the shops. The salespeople were very helpful and Mom got a nice coat, and the three of us enjoyed our time in the little village.

Not long after we got back, they were finally ready to begin boarding the ship. We all walked up the ramp together, expecting the usual "Welcome aboard!" and friendly faces. Instead what we got was an order to get out our passports and hand them over. It felt more like going through customs than boarding a vacation cruise. We had already showed our IDs to get on the ship, and here we were being asked for them again—although "asked" isn't really the appropriate word. I had never before had to turn over my passport on a cruise and I actually questioned the officer who asked me for it. I've always been told never to part with my passport because it is truly the *only* way to prove who you are while in another country. Several people from Europe who were behind us in line were concerned about having to part with their passports as well.

WE WERE EXPECTING THERE TO BE A MUSTER DRILL LATER THAT AFTERNOON, LIKE THERE HAD BEEN ON EVERY OTHER CRUISE WE HAD BEEN ON . . . WHEN WE LEARNED THERE WOULDN'T BE ONE THAT FIRST DAY, A HUGE RED FLAG WENT UP IN MY HEAD.

In answer to our concern, we were told that this was their policy and that our passports would be locked up and safe until the cruise was over. It wasn't very reassuring to me, but we really didn't have a choice. I've since learned that there are a handful of cruises, several of them in the Mediterranean (although not any we had ever been on), that follow this procedure, mainly to make it easier for the passengers to get off and on the ship at the various ports of call. But when you aren't warned about it ahead of time and it isn't clearly explained to you, it's alarming to hand over your passport to a total stranger. This whole process just didn't sit well with me.

By the time we were on the ship and heading to our cabins, our overall feeling was that this cruise line didn't care whether or not we ever cruised with them again. We were hoping the service would dramatically improve, but so far, we were not impressed.

Cindy and I were staying on a different deck than our parents, so we split up for a few minutes to drop off our carry-ons and see if our luggage had made it to our rooms yet. After that, we all met for lunch at the buffet on the top deck. Lunch was delicious and the staff there was very pleasant, so at least things were now improving.

Normally after we get on a cruise, we eat lunch and then head to our cabins to relax a little. We were expecting there to be a muster drill later that afternoon, like there had been on every other cruise we had been on. In fact, part of the reason we never plan anything for that first afternoon is because it's always inter-rupted by the muster drill, usually before we even leave the port. When we learned there wouldn't be one that first day, a huge red flag went up in my head. I had assumed that a muster drill was mandatory on the first day of a cruise, but apparently it wasn't. I asked when the drill would be and was told it was taking place the following day at 5:30 in the evening.

The point of a muster drill is for passengers and crew to go to their assigned muster stations so that they know exactly where to go and how to line up in the event there is a need to evacuate the ship. We had done dozens of these drills in our lives and it wasn't that I felt like I needed to do another one, but I knew there were probably many people on that ship who had never cruised before. I wondered if they would know where to go and what to do if something happened between when we left port and the next evening. I didn't have to wonder long.

Cindy and I headed to our room to take a nap since we didn't have to be up for the drill and we weren't eating dinner until 9:00 p.m. I decided to get some rest while Cindy did a little unpacking before she took a nap. Around 8:45 p.m., Cindy woke me up for dinner. She had taken a shower, but her hair was still wet.

Usually I'm the one that never dries my hair, so it's a family joke that if you wash your hair and run right out the door, you're "pulling a Val." She joked around about it when she woke me up, but luckily the first dinner on a cruise is pretty casual, so it was the perfect time to "pull a Val." Unfortunately, while wet hair and a casual spaghetti-strap tank top is perfectly fine for that first dinner, it's not very suitable for a late night escape from a sinking ship in January.

I was still pretty groggy from my nap and I told Cindy I didn't think I wanted to go to dinner since I was so exhausted and not at all hungry. I didn't want to be rude to the rest of the family, but I was still sleepy. Cindy told me not to worry about it since we would have plenty of dinners together in the days and weeks ahead, so I decided to just sit this one out and go back to sleep, even though I felt bad about it. That was about the time that Cindy discovered she couldn't find her ring.

Our Aunt Bessie, who is actually our great-aunt, had been to Greece the year before and had gotten all three of us girls matching rings, each of which had a Greek phrase on it indicating that it was for the protection of whomever was wearing it. Cindy had hers on before her shower and couldn't remember where she had put it. These rings have a lot of sentimental meaning to us, so I got out of bed to help her look for it; I finally found it in the bathroom. Cindy was relieved and by then I was wide awake, so I decided to join the family for dinner after all.

We were running behind thanks to the ring hunt, and then we got lost upon entering the massive two-story dining room, so we were pretty late for dinner by the time we finally found our parents. After apologizing for being so late, I noticed that our table was next to a group of young, rambunctious children who were sitting alone, with their parents sitting a few tables away. I love kids, which is probably why I'm an elementary school teacher, and I thought they were all so cute. Cindy, on the other hand, isn't such a fan of kids—especially loud, hyper kids. Yet Cindy's chair was conveniently the one closest to the table of kids—and our parents were just snickering away! She wouldn't have to sit next to the kids for very long though, since all hell was about to break loose.

- -

CHAPTER:

THREE

NAME:

DEAN

DATE:

1/13/12, 3:30PM–9:45PM CET

- -

Normally, when I travel and a major time difference is involved, I try to stay awake until it's time to go to bed so that I can get used to the new time zone as quickly as possible. But my blood pressure had been acting up on this trip and I was fatigued and didn't want to push myself too much on that first day. So when Georgia and I got back to our cabin after lunch, I decided to lie down and take a nap. I offered to help Georgia unpack before I fell asleep, but she told me to get some much-needed rest. I was so tired that I got in bed with my clothes on and my wallet and phone still in my pocket and fell right to sleep.

By the time I woke up around 7:30 that evening, my extremely efficient wife had everything unpacked and put away. She had even moved the room's three life jackets to the top of the closet, no small feat considering Georgia is pretty petite. Since the first night on a cruise is usually casual, I got out of bed and freshened up some, but I kept the same clothes on, which—in what would turn out to be a beneficial stroke of luck—still had everything in the pockets.

Georgia and I were on deck two and the restaurant was on decks three and four, and since we had a little time to kill before meeting the girls for dinner, we decided to wander around. I've been on a variety of cruise ships and they're all uniquely different. The outside of this ship wasn't anything to take note of, but the inside was pretty impressive. The décor was exquisite. Georgia and I always like to know where the Internet café is since that's where we check our email and keep in touch with the people back home, so we set off to search for it. We found it on the starboard (or right) side, close to the casino. We decided that after dinner we would go back to the Internet café and contact Debbie to let her know we had arrived safely. Then Georgia and I wandered through the casino and several of the other public rooms, just to get the lay of the land, so to speak. There was also a main staircase and a bank of elevators in the vicinity, which took us down to the restaurant where we would be having dinner. Most of the time, the dining rooms on ships are at the aft (or rear), on the lower levels, because that's the smoothest part of the ship. People couldn't enjoy their meals if the ship was swaying too much because of rough seas.

AT SOME POINT WHILE WE WERE SITTING IN THE DINING ROOM, THE THEME SONG FROM THE MOVIE *TITANIC* BEGAN PLAYING. I REMEMBER GEORGIA LOOKING AT ME AND COMMENTING THAT MAYBE THAT WASN'T THE BEST SONG TO PLAY ON A CRUISE SHIP. TURNS OUT SHE WAS MORE RIGHT THAN SHE KNEW.

As beautiful as the ship was, we never got to see much more than those couple of decks, since we weren't on the ship very long. Although within a couple of hours, I would have lost all desire to see any more of that ship than I had to.

Georgia and I got to our table ahead of the girls. Right away we noticed that the large table to one side of us was made up entirely of young kids whose parents were sitting a few tables away. It got even better when the waiter showed up with soda. "Holy smokes!" I told Georgia. "Look at this, now they've got caffeine! They'll behave really great tonight!" We couldn't let an opportunity like that go to waste, so I told Georgia to switch chairs to the other side of the table with me, next to a nice quiet couple, so that when the girls walked in, they'd be stuck sitting next to the kids. Before the girls arrived, at least one kid had already spilled his drink all over himself. The girls got to dinner around 9:20 and we ordered our appetizers and dinner. Cindy was thrilled with the seating arrangement, of course, and the rest of us couldn't help chuckling a little.

At some point while we were sitting in the dining room, the theme song from the movie *Titanic* began playing. I remember Georgia looking at me and commenting that maybe that wasn't the best song to play on a cruise ship. Turns out she was more right than she knew.

Sometime around 9:45, while we were eating our salads, we heard this rumbling sound. I wasn't too worried because we were sitting at the back of the ship, which is where the propellers (also called "screws") are located. The ship felt like it was turning. But then it started vibrating more, and one of the girls looked at me and said it felt like a mini earthquake, something we have all the time in California. As much as we were vibrating, I knew this had to be more than a simple turn. I was in the navy during the

Vietnam War so I'm pretty familiar with big ships and to me, it felt like the ship had been thrown into reverse. Since there are no brakes on a ship, when the bridge wants to stop, they have to throw it in reverse. About that time, I noticed the water in the glasses on the table was at a slight angle, which I thought must mean we were taking a hard turn, which is out of the ordinary for a big cruise ship.

Right then, we heard a loud bang and the lights flashed and pandemonium ensued. The guy next to us got up and bolted for the door with his wife hurrying to catch up to him. The table on the other side of us was a mess of hyper, screaming kids by now. Over the PA system, we heard an announcement, which at first we couldn't understand. After sitting through Italian, French, and German languages, we finally got to the English version and learned that we had "nothing to fear" because this was just an "electrical problem." The lights were still flashing on and off, and the ship was starting to list (slant) even more. My immediate reaction was that this was hardly just an electrical problem. I moved the family under the overhang from the balcony above since all kinds of things were starting to slide off that upper level and land all around us. I could tell the girls were worried, so I told them the ship was way too big to sink like a rock if we had hit anything; it would take quite a while to take down something of this size.

By this point, it wasn't just hyper kids who were screaming. The dining room was now filled with panicked passengers—pushing, shoving, trampling, and sliding their way out of the dining room. Dishes and silverware were falling from above and the slant was now enough that it was hard to walk without slipping. We decided to wait right where we were under the overhang until the stampede had cleared, to avoid getting trampled or separated in the crowd. We feared that leaving with the crowd might cause us to get hurt. Our family sticks together and works as a unit, and we weren't about to risk being split up.

CHAPTER:
FOUR

NAME:
CINDY

DATE:
1/13/12, 9:45PM–10:10PM CET

People were freaking out in various languages and everything was mass confusion. Dad had us huddled under the balcony to avoid the objects falling from above. As Californians, we're pretty good at knowing how to take cover when things start shaking and falling. It's Earthquake Survival 101. We tried to convince people to get under there with us, but between the language barriers and the panic, most people either couldn't understand us or were in a crazed state trying to escape from the dining room and just weren't thinking clearly. Panicking is the

THE SLIGHT SLANT WAS MAKING IT HARD TO WALK, LET ALONE RUN, SO PEOPLE WERE SLIDING AND FALLING AND TAKING OTHER PEOPLE DOWN WITH THEM.

worst thing you can do in a situation like that. And most people were doing exactly that.

There was a lot of screaming and yelling as people rushed for the doors. The slight slant was making it hard to walk, let alone run, so people were sliding and falling and taking other people down with them. Honestly though, at the time, no one knew how serious the situation was, so the running and screaming was a bit dramatic, and all it did was make the situation worse. Maybe it's because I'd never been afraid on a ship before, but I thought most people were massively overreacting. I just don't generally jump to the worst conclusion in a situation like that on a ship. Although I guess if something similar had happened on a plane, I would have immediately assumed we were going down! It's ironic that I'm so fear*ful* on a plane and so fear*less* on a ship.

In the midst of all of this hoopla, an announcement came on the PA system telling us that the problem was an electrical issue. While I understand that an electrical problem can cause the lights to go off and on, I was a little skeptical about how it would cause the ship to list at enough of an angle to where dishes were sliding off the tables. I couldn't think of an electrical problem that would cause that, but then I'm no electrician. Plus I was trying to give them the benefit of the doubt. However, right after the announcement, the ship shifted more, making it even less likely, in my mind, that this was electrical.

We figured we better get out of the dining room while walking was still doable. One of the waiters motioned for us to come and use a staff-only door and take the service stairs to the boat deck. The other exits were crammed with people and it would have taken us forever to get through that mess. So our family and a few others followed some of the waiters through the crew exit and made our way to the fourth deck, also known as the boat deck.

Things weren't much better up on the deck. Most people were still being more dramatic than I thought was really necessary. There was a lot of loud carrying-on, none of which was at all productive. I'm not exactly sure what was being said because very little of it was in English, but it's not hard to interpret yelling and crying. It was frustrating to watch because I don't generally like overly dramatic behavior like that. But again, if we'd been on a plane having issues, I'd have been the one panicking, so I guess I can sympathize with how they must have felt.

Because we hadn't had a muster drill, we didn't know where our muster station was. Normally on cruises, we get awakened from our naps to do the muster drill on that first day. They're mandatory, so if you don't go, you get nasty notes on your door and harassing messages from the crew until you make it up—which is a good thing because people need to know what to do in an emergency. Needless to say, as avid cruisers, we've reported to a *lot* of muster stations. We also knew the signal that meant "get your life jacket and go to your muster station." It's a series of short and long blasts so that there aren't any language issues. Crew members are usually spread out directing people to the stations, which are right next to the lifeboats. Once you get there, you line up and wait for directions from the crew member or officer assigned to your station. They tell you how your life jacket lights work and take attendance to make sure everyone is there and then they explain what would happen if there was a real emergency.

But none of that had happened on this cruise, so it didn't really matter which station we reported to. We also knew that since Val and I were assigned to a different deck than Mom and Dad, we would have different muster stations anyway and we had already decided there was no way we were splitting up. So for the time being we just stayed put, awaiting instructions. Around us was pure chaos. Maybe it was the lack of a drill or maybe it was just human nature, but there was absolutely zero order and organization to be had on deck. Sadly, people were still so panicked I'm not sure they could have lined up properly and followed procedure even if there had been an earlier drill.

Our family stayed huddled together taking in the mania. Mom was being uncharacteristically quiet and Val was being uncharacteristically assertive. Besides asking Dad (who had been in the navy) lots of questions, she was also trying to get information out of any crew member she could find, although none of them had been at all helpful or reassuring. They told her that this was all just an electrical problem caused by the generators and that everyone could go back to their rooms because they were in the process of fixing the problem. We could tell she was getting more and more frustrated by the complete disorganization, and finally she suggested that, no matter the outcome of this situation, we get off the ship at the very next port. She didn't trust the ship, the crew, or the way things were being run. Val has pretty good intuition about things and we usually trust her gut feelings. So we all agreed to cut this cruise short at the first opportunity. We figured we could tour Italy on land and then catch up with our next cruise. But we certainly weren't staying on this one.

Our family was fairly calm throughout this process, and we hadn't yet considered the possibility that our lives were in danger. Mom was still being pretty quiet, which was very unusual for her. Most of the time, my mom is a take-charge person, quick to come up with a plan and make sure we all carry it out. She's the decision-maker. But not this time. This time that job fell to Valerie. In most things, Valerie is very laid back and just goes with the flow. But when problems come up and things get intense, she becomes a different person and she's able to process bad situations quickly and think on her feet.

Val was convinced that we had hit something, especially since the ship kept shifting and listing more and more, the longer we stood there. She asked Dad how long he thought we'd have to get off the ship if it was sinking and at what point would we jump in and take our chances with the cold water.

A lot of the people around us were now using their phones to try to get ahold of loved ones, and many were taking pictures and video of the situation. Dad had his BlackBerry in his pocket, but he didn't have international service on it since we usually just go to the ship's Internet café and use the computers there if we need to communicate with someone at home. So even if we had wanted to, there was no way we could contact anyone to tell them what was going on.

After standing there for a while, waiting for something useful to happen, we noticed that everyone had on life jackets but us. Because we had stayed in the dining room until the stampede had passed, we were some of the last people up on the boat deck. Large bins that contained the life jackets were located on the deck, near the lifeboats. Apparently, before we had gotten up there, everyone had raided the bins and they were now totally empty. With this cruise, we knew one very important thing—we weren't getting on a lifeboat without a life jacket. And not a one of us had a life jacket. It seemed we had a real problem.

- -

CHAPTER:

FIVE

NAME:

GEORGIA

DATE:

1/13/12, 10:10PM–10:30PM CET

- -

We knew that the people manning the lifeboats weren't about to let us on a lifeboat without a life jacket. These people hadn't been trained on what to do in a situation like this, so all they knew to do was follow the instructions that had been given to them, even if they knew it might not be in the best interest of the passengers. I'd been on enough cruises to know that there are life jackets on the lifeboats, but this crew obviously wasn't aware of that. We tried to get them to grab several off of one of the boats for us, but they wouldn't listen. They were doing what they had been told to do or had practiced at previous muster drills and nothing else. It was clear that there was no way we were going to be allowed to evacuate the ship unless we could get our hands on four life jackets. It was also clear that we weren't going to get any help from the crew. I can't really blame them though. They tried their best, but they didn't have proper training, and they were just as scared as the passengers. You could see the terror in their eyes, even as they told us everything would be okay. They said it, but they didn't believe it.

COULD WE RISK GOING FURTHER DOWN INTO
THE SHIP TO GRAB THOSE JACKETS WHEN WE
DIDN'T KNOW IF IT WAS TAKING ON LARGE
AMOUNTS OF WATER? COULD WE RISK NOT
GOING AND BEING LEFT ON A SINKING SHIP?

By this point, I was becoming increasingly convinced that we needed to watch this crew closely since they were the ones that knew how to get off the ship and could possibly be the first ones off. I remembered hearing about a cruising accident in Africa where a Greek captain and some of the crew members got off the ship before any of the passengers had a chance to get off. I never actually dreamed that another captain would do that again, but I was worried that the same thing might happen here with the crew. I wanted everyone to pay close attention to how the crew members were acting and what they were doing since they knew the way off the ship better than we did.

The next problem we faced was the danger involved in going down to our deck to get life jackets out of the cabin. I had unpacked before dinner while Dean was resting and I knew exactly where the three from our cabin were, since I had moved them to the top of the closet myself. But the ship was starting to list more and more and walking was becoming very difficult. Could we risk going further down into the ship to grab those jackets when we didn't know if it was taking on large amounts of water? Could we risk not going and being left on a sinking ship?

By this time the emergency lighting was on, so we decided to take our chances and go get the life jackets out of our cabin. We didn't want to split up, especially since the girls' cabin was several decks away, but at least if we could get down to the deck Dean and I were on, three of us would have life jackets and maybe we could find another one somewhere else. So we got down on our hands and knees and crawled our way down two decks. In most places, it was too hard to see if we were standing up because the emergency lighting on a ship runs along the floor. And it was imperative for us to be able to see each other so that we didn't get separated. We had to go down a couple of staircases, which was not only difficult because of the lack of adequate lighting, but also because of the angle at which the boat was listing. It's harder than you think to walk or crawl down a flight of stairs when you are leaning to one side of the stairs!

Valerie told me later that she was almost expecting us to get down a deck or two and suddenly be sloshing through water. She didn't really believe the story about the electrical problem and already had an idea we might be sinking. So the whole time we were carefully making our way down, she was braced to encounter slowly rising water. I think her preparedness for that possibility just highlights again how little we all trusted in what the crew was telling us and how much we all thought something much more serious had to be wrong.

Finally, we made it down to the second deck—water-free, thank God. Dean had the key to the stateroom in his pocket and he was able to open the door in the little bit of light that was available. But inside, the room was pitch-black. Since I knew where the life jackets were, the girls and Dean stayed in the hall while I felt my way into the room and over to the closet. It was really eerie being in the room and not able to see anything. I knew it would take me forever to try to move a chair over to the closet and climb up in the dark, so I decided to just jump and grab and hope for the best. I managed to get all three of them pulled down that way, and I also fumbled my way around until I found the place where I knew I had left my purse and Dean's medication. Thank God I had unpacked right before dinner and remembered where I had put everything or there was no way I could have found what we needed in the dark.

Once I had everything, I carefully made my way back to the door and headed out to where the family was waiting for me in the hall. I think my ability to maneuver around so quickly happened because of my familiarity with different cruise staterooms on other cruises. Seeing my family when I left the cabin was a welcomed sight after being in a pitch-black room where I could easily have been trapped.

Just as I came out into the hallway though, I saw a room steward walking towards us. I remember feeling so relieved because, not only were we still one life jacket short, but I had noticed that one of the three we had was smaller and for a child. The girls are petite enough that I knew one of them could use the child's life jacket if necessary (probably Valerie since she's the strongest swimmer of all of us), but either way, we were still one short. I knew that room stewards had master keys to get into all the cabins, and I asked him to open another cabin for us so that we could grab one or two more life jackets. Just in case he didn't speak English, I showed him what we had and motioned with my hands that we were one short. Shockingly, he told us no, he "wasn't allowed" to let us in another cabin to get them out, nor would he go in and get one for us. I tried to explain that he *needed* to help us, but he was adamant that he wasn't opening any doors for us.

It honestly felt like that horrible scene in the movie *Titanic* where the people in steerage are trying to get the steward to unlock the gate and let them up to the boat deck so they can get on the lifeboats, but he won't because he "isn't allowed" to open the gate. We knew we needed a fourth life jacket to get off the ship and we knew there were life jackets in every single stateroom, but here was a steward who refused to help us because policy told him he couldn't unlock the doors for passengers to get in someone else's cabin. It was surreal. And we didn't have time to argue with him because we needed to get back up on deck. Dean was behind the girls when this happened and didn't hear my conversation with the room steward, but he told me later that if he'd been aware of it, he probably would have just knocked him out and taken his key! That just shows how desperate we were by that point.

We started making our way back up to the boat deck. We had looked everywhere on our way down to the cabin for any life jackets and hadn't been able to find any. I was starting to get really worried about us being one short. Not only could it mean that one of us wouldn't be allowed on a lifeboat by these by-the-book crew members, but if we found ourselves in the position of needing to jump overboard, one of us wouldn't have a life jacket in that cold water. And at this point, we had no idea how close to land we were. In fact, because of the side of the ship we were on, it looked to us like we were in the middle of the ocean! Not a good place to be without a life jacket.

And then there it was. I was making my way back up onto the fourth deck when I saw a gray life jacket right in front of me. Not a single person was nearby and I *know* it hadn't been there when we had headed down the stairs. So I dove forward and grabbed it. It was damp and didn't look a thing like the orange life jackets that everyone else had. All I know is that it hadn't been there a few minutes earlier when we'd made our way down. I realize that not everyone believes in miracles, but in that instant, I most certainly did. All four people in my family had a life jacket and I could breathe easier.

- -

CHAPTER:

S I X

NAME:

D E A N

DATE:

1/13/12, 10:30PM–11:00PM CET

- -

By the time we got back on deck, the ship was listing notice-ably, and I was pretty sure we were taking on large amounts of water. If it were anything else, the stabilizers would be cor-recting the list. Most cruise ships have these wing-like extensions on the outside at the water level called stabilizers, enabling them to glide smoothly along. Basically, they're kind of like the flaps on airplanes and are used to correct the normal rolling of the ship caused by waves. But this list hadn't been corrected and the only thing I could think of was that we had hit something hard enough to create a major breach on one side of the ship.

Even then, I couldn't understand why the pumps were not doing their job to get the water back out. Big ships can usually take on some amount of water, thanks to pumps that push the water back out and make it feasible to get back to port safely. If we were taking in water, the pumps should have been working to keep the water distributed evenly and as much pumped out of the ship as possible. Unfortunately, it seemed at that time that the main generators were not functioning and, as I later learned, the backup generators only ran the emergency lights, not the pumps.

I knew that the lower compartments of a ship are vacuum-sealed and thus able to contain some water without affecting the rest of the ship. I heard later that at least two of these compartments could have been flooded and the ship would have stayed afloat; apparently we had three of them breached. But at the time, I didn't know how many compartments were flooded, the real state of the generators, or even that we were for sure taking on water. I just knew something had to be terribly wrong for us to be listing like that.

Our family was on the port side of the ship, facing out to sea with the ship listing towards the water. Everyone on that side thought we were in the middle of the ocean since all we could see was water. Once we all had life jackets, our family had returned to our position up against the bulkhead (or wall) at the nearest muster station. I remember later seeing video of the scene on deck, with everyone waiting for the abandon-ship signal to be given. I was shocked by all the yelling and screaming because I didn't remember hearing any of it at the time. I guess I had gone into some kind of survival mode and blocked out the distractions around us, like a relief pitcher does in a baseball game. He blocks out all the noise in order to concentrate on pitching in the midst of thousands of screaming fans. I think the girls might have been more aware of the noise than I was. I know Cindy and Val were pretty frustrated by the disorganization and drama.

The crew wasn't helping the situation, and I started to worry that even if we were finally put on the lifeboats, the crew members wouldn't know how to run them. Most of them were waiters and kitchen staff, and I highly doubted they had been trained on how to man a lifeboat. These lifeboats aren't just big rowboats—they're like large motorboats, which are fairly tall and have engines.

We had been trying to convince the crew that we needed to board the lifeboats sooner rather than later, but the captain still had not given the signal to abandon ship, and they certainly weren't going to start boarding until they were told to, regardless of how bad the situation looked. Valerie specifically kept at them, trying to get them to understand that we really needed to start putting people on the lifeboats. If they had started loading the lifeboats when everyone had first gone on deck, I have no doubt everyone would have safely gotten off the ship without incident. But no signal came and this crew was too scared to do anything other than follow directions.

THE GATES TO THE LIFEBOATS WERE FINALLY OPENED AND MANY PASSENGERS MADE A MAD DASH TO BOARD THEM, SHOVING OTHERS ASIDE AND BASICALLY JUMPING INTO THE BOATS. WE GOT ON ONE AND TOOK OUR SEATS, RELIEVED THAT WE WERE SAFE AND THAT THE NIGHTMARE WAS OVER. BUT THE NIGHTMARE WAS JUST BEGINNING.

At some point, after we had been waiting on the deck for quite some time, the ship suddenly took a dramatic roll and we all grabbed to keep our footing as the slant flipped towards the starboard side. This only served to create more panic and pandemonium. Now, instead of leaning towards the water, we were leaning in towards the bulkheads. This would soon create a problem for the lifeboats, which needed to be lowered into the water.

Finally we heard the signal to abandon ship—several short blasts and one long blast. I don't remember ever hearing anything on the PA system, but we knew what the blasts meant, so we knew it was finally time to abandon ship. What we didn't know, and learned later, was that the captain got off the ship soon after he gave the abandon-ship signal. He later claimed he was "thrown" off the ship and landed in a lifeboat, but I find that highly unlikely—especially considering he refused to reboard the ship when he was ordered to do so by the Coast Guard.

We felt a sense of relief when the abandon-ship signal was given and we were very anxious to load the lifeboats. I remember hearing that the lifeboats could still be lowered as long as the ship was not listing more than twenty degrees, so at this point, our angle must have been slightly less than that. The gates to the lifeboats were finally opened and many passengers made a mad dash to board them, shoving others aside and basically jumping into the boats. We got on one and took our seats, relieved that we were safe and that the nightmare was over. But the nightmare was just beginning.

CHAPTER:

SEVEN

NAME:

VALERIE

DATE:

1/13/12, 11:00PM–11:20PM CET

Before we started boarding the lifeboats, there was an ineffective attempt to line everyone up. It was unfortunate that most people were still too panicked, and since the crew was so disorganized, they had no luck establishing any sort of order. As soon as the gates were opened to the boats, there was screaming and shoving as everyone fought to get a spot on a lifeboat. I had been talking to a crew member for a while before the abandon-ship signal was given, explaining how urgent it was that we begin boarding the lifeboats. My fear was that, by the time they finally got us all on, the angle of the ship would be too great to lower the boats.

He understood what I was saying, but since the captain hadn't given the signal, he had to just follow orders. He tried to be comforting though, and he took my hand and told me not to worry, that everything would be okay. I tried to explain that I wasn't worried for myself so much as worried that *everyone* on this side of the ship would be stranded if we waited too long and the lifeboats couldn't be lowered. I was very adamant about how dangerous it was to keep waiting, but he just kept reassuring me that everything would be fine. I'm not sure whether he wasn't aware of how bad things were or whether he was just downplaying the situation to keep people calm.

Since I had been up there talking to him, when they finally opened our gate, we were fortunately some of the first passengers on that lifeboat. I had already decided that, with this crowd, we were going to have to be assertive about getting seats on the lifeboat because, otherwise, we might get shoved aside or trampled. Once we were on the lifeboat, I felt a little better, but I knew I wouldn't breathe easier until the boat was lowered down to the water. The ship had been listing more and more while we waited to board and I had this bad feeling that, when the time came, they wouldn't be able to lower us because the side of the ship would be in the way. I was concerned that the list was already too great—it just didn't make sense to me how we would be able to get down the side without scraping along the ship and risking tipping the lifeboat.

For some reason, it took longer to load our lifeboat, so most of the other boats on our side were already being lowered into the water. Luckily, they were making sure to fill up our boat, which is definitely better than sending it down half-empty, but it seemed to be taking an eternity to get everyone on board. There was an Argentinian couple with a little girl, probably around two or three years old, sitting near us. I'm by no means fluent in Spanish, but I do speak and understand enough that I could converse with them while we waited. I learned that the woman was a teacher and that the daughter's name was Valentina, which struck me because of its similarity to my name. The dad was bouncing Valentina on her knee, trying to keep her calm. It made my heart break to look at this cute, innocent little girl, especially since I still wasn't confident that this boat would get us safely off the ship.

It bothered me greatly to see such a young child in such a scary situation, with people screaming and crying all around her. It had to be terrifying for her since she probably didn't understand what was going on. Most of the adults on board were acting more terrified than the children. One older lady, who was very distraught, slipped and fell near us as she was getting on and we had to help her up and try to calm her down some, but she just kept sobbing and crying hysterically.

To make matters worse, a female crew member, dressed all in white, got on with us as the boat was still filling up and rudely yelled that everyone needed to turn off their phones and cameras and stop filming. I'm not sure whether she was told to say that or whether she just took it upon herself to give the order. She also decided she needed us to count ourselves off while we waited to be lowered down to the water. For the life of me, I still can't figure out what purpose this could have served. It seemed so unnecessary and useless since she wanted us to count in English and most people on the ship didn't speak English. We could barely get through a few numbers when someone would get lost and not know what number came next. I tried to help some of the people around us, but the process just wasn't working very well because the passengers were confused and distraught.

Maybe we would have understood the system if we had done a muster drill; it's possible that's how things were done on this cruise line. Since we hadn't practiced anything like this before and only a small fraction of the passengers spoke English, all it served to do was waste more precious time. I don't know whether we would have been able to lower the boat if we hadn't spent so much time attempting to number ourselves, but at least we would have had a better chance. Everyone was still so upset, and I couldn't shake my intuitive feeling that this wasn't going to work out in our favor.

Finally, they started trying to lower our boat. I remember my heart was pounding and I was so excited, hoping that we would make it to the water, but I wasn't willing to believe it until we were actually down there. As we were being lowered, a man tried to jump from the ship to the lifeboat. By this time, there was a gap between us and the ship as we were being moved out and down. There were these long metal rails that stuck out from the ship, which were used to move the lifeboats out so that they could be dropped down. The man tried to get on our boat by jumping out to one of these rails and using it to climb on board, but the people on the boat had to stop him before he capsized us or slipped and fell through. It was terrifying to witness a person in such desperation.

He did not miss out on much by not getting on the lifeboat though, because as they tried to lower us, the boat hit and scraped against the side of the ship. They made several attempts, using a long pole to try to push us far enough away to get down safely, but each attempt just resulted in more scraping, and the danger of the boat flipping over was just too great. Eventually someone yelled out "Stop! Stop!" And I knew right that very instant that we weren't going to make it to the water. Instead of being safely on our way to shore and finished with this horrific night, we now had to evacuate the lifeboat and get back on board the sinking cruise ship. It felt like my heart shattered into a thousand pieces—if we couldn't get off the ship on a lifeboat, what would we do now?

CHAPTER:

EIGHT

NAME:

GEORGIA

DATE:

1/13/12, 11:00PM–11:20PM CET

We were well over an hour into this ordeal, still standing around on deck amidst confused, scared people and equally confused, scared crew members, and we had yet to see a single officer. In fact, most of the crew around us were kitchen staff— cooks, waiters, dishwashers. It was obvious that these people had not been given any training on how to corral hundreds of panicked passengers. When the signal was finally given to evacuate the ship and they opened the gates to the lifeboats, all hell broke loose. People trampled and stomped and shoved other people trying to get on the boats. I remember thinking, "Oh my God, we'll die before we get on the lifeboat at this rate." Our family isn't the type to push past other people to save ourselves first, so we were at a significant disadvantage. Thankfully, we had made a quick friendship with a nice crewman and he helped us out, so we were able to get on a boat without any major difficulties. I think he felt sorry for the girls because they had asked him so many times to please get our family on a lifeboat.

There had been very little organization leading up to the

abandon-ship signal. In some areas, there were approximately five hundred people waiting at the gate of one lifeboat—not very practical since most lifeboats only hold around one hundred and fifty people. Once boarding started, people were running and jumping on whatever boat they could get on, panicked that the boats would fill up before they could find one to get on board. We were sitting near a window on our boat, waiting for everyone else to get on and watching the pandemonium outside. There was an Argentinian couple with a baby next to us and we struck up a conversation with them, in our broken Spanish and their broken English. I was feeling pretty happy at this point—I was on a lifeboat and I could see the end of this nightmare in sight. There had been so many times I didn't think we'd get on a lifeboat that just being on one made it easier to relax and chat with the people around us. We learned that the Argentinian woman was a math teacher, which we identified with as a family full of educators. The family seemed to be very loving and caring to the daughter, who was clinging to her dad in desperation. She tried to hide her head under her dad's face so that she didn't have to see what was going on.

Suddenly, a woman who obviously worked for Costa came on the lifeboat and promptly informed us that we needed to start counting. She began with the people nearest her and had them number themselves as one, two, three, and so on, like you might do with a group of young children on a field trip. Unfortunately, most people on the cruise were Italian and didn't speak English, so having them try to count themselves off in English only created more confusion. When people would mess up, she'd start the whole process over again, as if somehow everyone would have learned their English numbers by the time she got back around to them. I couldn't figure out what we were doing counting instead of getting the lifeboat down to the water and heading away from the ship.

In the midst of the counting fiasco, people were trying to leap onto the lifeboat, which was still level with the deck, but had been moved out over the water in preparation for lowering. It was terrifying to see people being pushed back as they try to jump on, wondering if they'd fall through or get hurt. Several people had their phones or cameras out and one man was taking pictures of everything happening on the lifeboat and the deck. Apparently this didn't sit well with the Costa employee (the one leading the counting) because as soon as she saw it, she immediately stopped the numbering and rushed over to him and demanded that he put his camera away.

A German lady, somewhat older, was shoved onto the life-boat and just about fell on top of us. She sat down with our family and we tried to talk to her but she was frantic and crying hysterically. We kept telling her everything would be okay, but she couldn't seem to calm down. By now, the counting woman had taken up her post at the front again and was starting back up with our numbering. It seemed like things went on this way for close to half an hour, with her having us count, start over, count again, stop someone with a camera, count again—and on and on. The whole thing seemed like a bad joke—like we had somehow become unwitting actors in a farce or a Shakespearean comedy. Valerie, being a teacher, finally had enough and tried to help people by telling them what number to say, thinking maybe if we could finish with the ridiculous numbering, they would finally lower us down.

I don't think we ever officially finished counting ourselves off, but eventually they did start the winches, which would lower us down. Unfortunately, they couldn't get us very far because of the angle of the ship. Never had I considered that they wouldn't be able to get the lifeboat down to the water. But apparently the ship had been listing more and more. Since we were suspended out over the side, we couldn't feel the angle increasing, but it must have gotten bad enough to make it impossible to launch the boat. They spent ten or fifteen minutes trying to get us out far enough to lower us down, but finally they gave up, used the winches to bring us back up to deck level, and told us to get out of the lifeboat.

IT WAS SO HARD TO LISTEN TO OTHER PEOPLE SCREAMING AND CRYING AND KNOW THAT MANY OF THEM WERE HURT. BUT I REMEMBER SAYING TO MYSELF, "GEORGIA, AS MUCH AS YOU LOVE PEOPLE, YOU'RE NEVER GOING TO BE ABLE TO HELP ALL OF THEM HERE."

Obviously, people who have fled a sinking ship and finally made it to a lifeboat don't exactly want to get off that lifeboat and back onto the sinking ship. So when we weren't getting off fast enough for them, they started grabbing and yanking and shoving us back onto the ship. Since the deck was now sharply angled away from us, when I was thrown off the lifeboat, I slid all the way across and slammed hard into the bulkhead! It's a wonder I wasn't seriously hurt. And I wasn't the only one that this happened to. The incline was so great now that it had created a slide of sorts from the lifeboats to the interior deck wall so that when you stepped (or got shoved) off the lifeboat, it was too steep to stand and people just went sliding down, straight into the wall or anyone who happened to be in front of the wall. Several people were injured. I saw one woman severely twist her ankle, but there was no way to help her because it was now too difficult to stand, let alone assist someone else, which is my natural instinct.

It was so hard to listen to other people screaming and crying and know that many of them were hurt. But I remember saying to myself, "Georgia, as much as you love people, you're never going to be able to help all of them here." I knew I had to shut out the cries and everything around me and concentrate on what to do next and how to save my family. From that moment on, I was able to focus on what we had to do and tune out all the terror and panic around me. Up until then, all I could hear was screaming and crying, but once I made myself direct my thoughts and energy to getting my family off that ship, everything else just faded away to dead silence. Dean describes it as what happens to a pitcher in a baseball game. I haven't played a lot of baseball, so I can't know for sure, but I do know that after that, my brain refused to accept the noise and distractions around me. I didn't know the brain was capable of being that totally focused.

CHAPTER:

NINE

NAME:

DEBBIE

DATE:

1/13/12, 5:45PM EST

I had been in Miami since Wednesday, enjoying some girl time and relaxing after the last busy four months. Thursday, Mom called me from the airport in LA to tell me that Dad's blood pressure was elevated. She said she might need me to call our family doctor and get prescriptions sent to Italy if it didn't improve. I'd told her that would not be a problem, that I would just need the pharmacy information, and I would take care of everything. I wasn't completely aware at the time of how high his blood pressure was. They later told me that they had considered not even getting on the plane to Rome because of their concerns.

Although I was a little alarmed at the time, I thought if we could get his medicine sent to him in Rome, everything would be fine. I did worry about why his blood pressure was up suddenly, out of nowhere, when it had been fine throughout the busy wedding planning. I didn't think it would go up just because of the trip. My dad is the most calm, non-anxious person I know. Nothing about flying or traveling ever bothers him. Normally it's Cindy that I worry about when it comes to traveling on a

I WAS OUT SHOPPING WITH A GIRLFRIEND WHEN, SUDDENLY, I GOT THIS WEIRD UNPLEASANT FEELING AND REALIZED I HAD NEVER HEARD BACK FROM MY FAMILY AFTER THEY ARRIVED IN ROME.

plane because she's really scared of flying. In fact, I usually sit with Cindy when we fly to help her calm down. But Dad is really laid back about flights and cruises (in fact, he sleeps straight through most flights), so I didn't think his blood pressure was related to the trip.

Mom had called again, this time from Atlanta, but didn't have much time to chat because of a complicated gate change and a short layover, so we had quickly agreed that she would email me once they got on the ship. But a day had passed and it was now Friday afternoon. I was out shopping with a girlfriend when, suddenly, I got this weird unpleasant feeling and realized I had never heard back from my family after they arrived in Italy. After calculating the time difference in my head, I figured they had to be on the ship by then, and they usually would have emailed me right away. When I said something to my friend about it, she commented on how odd it was, since my mom is usually so on top of things and contacts me as soon as she has a chance.

I decided to send Mom an email from my phone to briefly tell her that I hadn't heard back from her and didn't know what was going on and was a little apprehensive. I still couldn't put my finger on why I had such a strange feeling. I don't know what it was, but I really thought something might be wrong. Normally Mom is really good about emailing when she says she's going to, especially since she knew I was concerned about Dad. My parents always set up an Internet package when they cruise so that we can communicate with the family while we're gone. So I knew she *would* email, I just didn't know why she hadn't yet. Something about the whole situation didn't feel right to me.

CHAPTER:

TEN

NAME:

DEAN

DATE:

1/13/12, 11:20PM–11:40PM CET

We had made our way below deck on a dark, listing ship for our life jackets; waited around amidst the pandemonium of screaming, crying, and panicking people on deck; and maneuvered our way onto a lifeboat—but it had all been for nothing. We were back on a ship that was clearly going down and it didn't look like there was any way off.

It's difficult to picture what it's like to be on a massive cruise ship that is leaning to one side unless you've been on one. And even then, it can be very disorienting. We seemed to be slanting more than twenty degrees because it had been impossible to launch the lifeboat. Twenty degrees doesn't sound like a lot, but when you consider that the average roof is usually slanted less than that (and how difficult it is to walk on a roof), it starts to make a little more sense why people were having such a hard time keeping their footing. To make matters worse, ship decks are made of steel that can be fairly slick when wet. So basically what you have when you slant the deck at any substantial angle is a slide—a slide with hundreds of panicked people on it and no obvious way off.

Aside from our trek down to get the life jackets, we had been on the boat deck, or deck four, throughout this entire ordeal. The boat deck has all the lifeboats lined up down the outside of it. They sit along the deck on long metal beams, which are used to winch the boats out and suspend them over the side for lowering into the water. Once the lifeboats had been launched, the exterior side of the deck had large empty gaps where the boats had been, and the long metal beams stuck randomly out from the deck. Slant the whole thing at a precarious angle and deck four now had the makings to be a dangerous obstacle course.

Further down the deck and in between the bulkhead and where the lifeboats had been along the outside ran a short interior railing attached to a stairwell that went down to the deck below. There were also several doors along the wall, where we were, that had swung open because of the angle. So we were leaning up against a wall with openings on one side of us, a short railing in the middle of the deck, and big gaps and metal beams on the far side of the deck.

Due to the list, everyone had basically fallen and slid into the bulkhead after getting off the lifeboat, so there were now over a hundred people smashed up against the wall. Many people had gotten hurt crashing into the bulkhead. Many of the women who had been wearing heels had taken them off earlier because it was too dangerous to walk in them on such a slant. A lot of those women had then cut their feet during the slide and subsequent collision with the wall and each other. And now that our lifeboat was non-functioning (as far as actually being able to get us off the ship), no one knew exactly where to go or what to do.

At this point, Georgia threw her purse on the deck so she could better handle balancing herself on the severely listing deck. I had no idea how many people were stuck on that port side with us at the time, but I heard later that there were roughly a thousand people stranded on that side of the ship when the list became too great to launch the lifeboats. The problem with being stuck on the port side was that we couldn't even jump off into the water. At least the people on the starboard side were slowly getting closer and closer to the water as the ship turned on her side, so eventually they could jump in and swim for it. Of course, they could also see that land was only a short distance away, whereas we still thought we were in the middle of the ocean.

WE HAD ONLY MANAGED TO INCH FORWARD ABOUT A THIRD OF THE WAY DOWN THE HALLWAY WHEN WE STARTED HEARING GLASSES BREAKING AND PLATES CRASHING. THEN ALL AT ONCE WE FELT THE SHIP ROLL OVER EVEN MORE, AND THE INCLINE GOT EVEN STEEPER.

After much confusion and sliding around, everyone managed to line up against the wall and start inching back towards the stern (or rear) of the ship. There was a doorway up ahead to a corridor that cut directly across the ship and came out on the starboard side, where we were told we could still get another lifeboat so we could get off the ship. Big cruise ships have these cross-hallways connecting the left and right sides of the ship, basically as shortcuts from one side to the other. It took a while for the big group of us to shuffle along the bulkhead until we got to the door to the corridor. Standing at the doorway was one of the ship's cooks (which was pretty obvious since he was still wearing his chef's hat) and he told us there were boats being launched off the other side. If we could get there in time, we might still be able to get a spot on one. So we followed everyone else into the dark hallway, hoping for the best.

Once we turned down the hallway, we essentially were headed straight down a pitch-black ramp, with a small light way up ahead—our proverbial light at the end of the tunnel. And we had to get to that light if we wanted off this ship. Luckily, there was a fairly good-sized chair rail running along the wall of the corridor so we were able to hang on to that as we inched along. It helped that the hallway was carpeted, so our feet had a little more traction than they'd had on the slick deck. But as anyone who has ever walked down a steep hill knows, traction doesn't help much when your balance is off.

We also didn't know what we were walking into. Would we get halfway down the corridor and wind up with wet feet because the boat was tipped so far over in the water? Would we get to the starboard side before the last boats were launched? Would we have to jump overboard and hope a boat picked us up before hypothermia set in? The only way to get answers was to keep heading down towards the tiny little light at the other end of the tunnel. We had only managed to inch forward about a third of the way down the hallway when we started hearing glasses breaking and plates crashing. Then all at once we felt the ship roll over even more, and the incline got even steeper. Ahead of us, we could hear people screaming, along with the sounds of more dishes smashing into the floor. Clearly it wasn't safe to continue to the other side, so I stopped the family and told them we had to get out of there and get back outside and up to the highest part of the ship. It looked like getting off the ship on a lifeboat just wasn't in the cards for us that night.

- -

CHAPTER:

ELEVEN

NAME:

CINDY

DATE:

1/13/12, 11:40PM–1/14/13 12:00AM CET

- -

I had been skeptical about going down the hallway to the other side of the ship for a couple of reasons. First, I couldn't see how it could be safe, since the ship was seriously leaning that way and I figured there had to be water near or above the deck level on the starboard side by now. And second, it didn't make sense to me that there would be enough room on those lifeboats for all of

IT WAS FAR TOO RISKY TO KEEP MOVING DEEPER INTO THE SHIP, WHICH WAS NOW DANGEROUSLY CLOSE TO BEING ON ITS SIDE. EVERY MINUTE, WE WERE EXPECTING WATER TO COME RUSHING UP; WE KNEW WE HAD TO FIND A WAY TO GET TO A HIGHER POINT BEFORE THAT HAPPENED.

us who were stranded on the port side. Cruise ships have enough lifeboat space for everyone on board, and probably some extra space, but I didn't think there would be *enough* extra space in the boats to accommodate everyone on the starboard side as well as at least several hundred people from where we were. That just didn't make sense to me.

As we were making our way down the corridor, I remember seeing a guy next to me who clearly worked on the ship. I asked him if he knew what was going on and if he thought we were going to list any more. I thought he might know more than some of the other crew because he seemed to be a maintenance worker or something, based on the jumpsuit he was wearing. Most of the other crew members we had talked to were kitchen workers or waitstaff, so I was hoping that this man might have a better idea of our situation than they did. He was very sweet and patted my hand and told me not to worry, that the ship shouldn't move anymore. Valerie asked him if he was *sure* the ship wouldn't flip over and he assured us that it was stable now. I let myself believe him and thanked him for reassuring me. But my happy feelings were short-lived.

Within minutes of this conversation, we heard a deafening noise as more of the plates started crashing to the floor. Immediately following this we took the most dramatic roll of the night and everyone screamed and grabbed for the railing, hoping to stay upright and not go careening down the hallway to the far deck. The force of the roll was so great that I thought we were about to completely capsize. Dad told us there was no way we could keep going down towards the starboard side, and we knew he was right. It was far too risky to keep moving deeper into the ship, which was now dangerously close to being on its side. Every minute, we were expecting water to come rushing up; we knew we had to find a way to get to a higher point before that happened.

When you're moving down a very steep hill (especially a hill that just got exponentially steeper while you were on it), it's incredibly hard to stop your forward motion and turn around. Momentum and gravity are working together to keep you moving downward, so it takes every ounce of energy and all your leg strength to fight back and work against the force. But we had to get back up on deck, so we grabbed the handrail, firmly planted ourselves, and inched our way around, then we leaned into the hill to climb our way back up.

We weren't yet halfway through the corridor when we turned around, so we didn't have to climb too terribly far. I know that several of the people farther in than we were also came back up to the port deck, but I don't know what happened to those who were deeper into the hallway. I don't know whether they were thrown down to whatever waited on the starboard side, whether they decided to take their chances and keep moving down on their own accord, or whether they eventually fought their way back to the port side like we did. It was so dark and we were concentrating so hard on staying upright at this point, that it was difficult to know what was going on around us. It's haunting, though, to think about all those other people in the hallway and not know what happened to them.

The climb back up to the deck was physically exhausting. Picture one of those steep concrete highway embankments and then imagine trying to walk up it with nothing but a chair rail to hang on to. And if anyone in that hallway lost his or her footing and fell backwards, that person would create a domino effect, taking out all the people down the line. Because of the angle, we were almost positive that the starboard side of the boat had to be partially submerged in the cold water. It was crucial that everyone move slowly and not fall.

Finally, we emerged back on the deck. Before we had started down the corridor, the list had turned the deck into a slide. But when we got back up there, the most recent roll of the ship had turned the deck into a wall and the wall had become the floor. We had to pull ourselves back out of the hallway and stand on what was technically the bulkhead (but was now functioning as the floor), looking at the deck in front of us, which stuck up into the sky. About nine or ten feet up the deck was a railing, which ran a short distance along the middle of the deck and down a random stairwell. We thought if we could get up on this middle railing, we could either see where the stairs led or possibly get to the outer railing of the ship and make our way to higher ground.

I'M INCREDIBLY PROUD OF MYSELF AND OF MY FAMILY THAT WE NEVER LET FEAR OF INJURY OR SELF-DOUBT KEEP US FROM TACKLING ANYTHING THAT STOOD BETWEEN US AND SURVIVAL.

No one in our family is exceptionally tall, so the railing wasn't easily accessible. But I thought if the rest of them could help me get up there, I could in turn help pull them up. I told the family to push me up so that I could grab onto the railing and hoist myself through. They all got behind me and shoved me up the deck. I grasped onto two of the rails and managed to drag myself the rest of the way. I felt like a kid on the monkey bars, hanging on with my hands and swinging my feet up and through to get to the top.

Once I was on the other side of the railing and looking back down, I leaned as far through as I could and told my mom and sister, "Give me your hand!" I had more leverage being above them so it was easier for me to help pull them up from below. Once I got Val up there with me (she used the same monkey-bar technique that I did), we both pulled Mom up. We didn't think we could get Dad up there, so he told us to get to the side, out of the way, and he would jump for it. Once we were clear, he squatted down low and then leapt up (almost like a frog), grabbed ahold of the rails, and pulled himself up and over.

Looking back, it's amazing to me some of the physical feats we were able to accomplish that night. Getting back up that hallway and up onto the railing was definitely not the most difficult thing we would do, but it certainly wasn't easy. Everyone in our family is in decent shape, but by no means are any of us extreme athletes. We don't go mountain climbing or tackle obstacle courses or anything like that. So to be in a situation where we were constantly being challenged physically, at the same time that we were dealing with the mental and emotional realities of being on a sinking ship, was a little crazy. Surprisingly though, we managed to take on every physical obstacle we were faced with, no matter how impossible it seemed. And I'm incredibly proud of myself and of my family that we never let fear of injury or self-doubt keep us from tackling anything that stood between us and survival.

CHAPTER:

TWELVE

NAME:

VALERIE

DATE:

1/14/12, 12:00AM–12:20AM CET

Once we were all balanced up on the railing, looking down at the bulkhead below us (much like Jack and Rose in *Titanic* right before it takes its final dive into the ocean), we turned our attention to the stairwell. I think we had all been desperately hoping that we could get down the stairs to the deck below and find some exit that would take us straight to the water level and we could just swim for it. One of the passengers who had climbed up to the railing with us was closer to the stairs and went down to check if there was an exit. Once he got down there though, he yelled back up that there was no way out. I didn't want to believe it could possibly be a dead end, so I held on tightly to the railing and leaned as far down the stairwell as I could, only to learn that he was right—there was no way out. I guess it was some sort of maintenance stairwell for crew and only they had access to it, and there was no crew around.

As time went by, the darkness seemed more intense and I kept wondering whether this was a sign of our impending demise. I'm not sure whether the recent roll had taken out more of the emergency lights, or whether I was just then noticing the darkness, but I have this memory of looking around at that point and realizing how despairingly dark it was. We were all certain that the ship would continue its death roll into the sea any minute, and we could see no way to safely even get into the water, let alone onto a lifeboat. You could tell that everyone on that railing and in that stairwell suddenly realized just how desperate our situation was.

HE KNEW THAT THE SHIP WAS ROLLING OVER.
HE KNEW THAT WE COULDN'T JUMP BECAUSE OF
THE ANGLE. HE KNEW THAT WHEN WE FINALLY
CAPSIZED, WE WOULD BE TRAPPED UNDERWATER
WITH A CRUISE SHIP FORCING US DOWN IN
A RAPID DIVE TO THE BOTTOM OF THE SEA.
AND I REALIZED THEN THAT ALL OF HIS
EXPERIENCE WAS TELLING HIM ONE THING—
THIS WAS THE END.

It was also about this time that I noticed my mom, who was on the other side of Cindy, was holding a child. When I looked, I saw that it was the little Argentinian girl from the lifeboat, the one with the name like mine—Valentina. Her parents had made it up to the railing behind us, and I guess the father had handed my mom the baby for some reason. My mom is of small stature and I was worried that she wouldn't be able to hang on to this little girl and still cling to the railing—I didn't want both of them to fall through.

It was then that I looked at my dad, the veteran, who I had been pelting with questions throughout this entire ordeal, hoping that his navy experience and knowledge of ships would somehow be enough to save us. But what I saw in him was heartbreaking.

WE TALKED AND PRAYED ON THAT RAILING, WAITING FOR THE WATER TO COME, WAITING TO DIE.

I had obviously already known we were in a dire situation, but seeing the look on my dad's face made it all the more real. He knew that the ship was rolling over. He knew that we couldn't jump because of the angle. He knew that when we finally capsized, we would be trapped underwater with a cruise ship forcing us down in a rapid dive to the bottom of the sea. And I realized then that all of his experience was telling him one thing—this was the end.

I could tell he was trying to be strong and not worry us, and he kept patiently answering every question I threw at him. But the look on his face said more than his verbal answers, and we all realized the truth. When my mom knew the end was near, she handed the baby back to the couple so that they could be with their daughter and we huddled together as best as we could on the railing. I started saying The Creed, a Greek Orthodox prayer we knew by heart and had said so many times in church. It was comforting to say the words together one last time.

We talked and prayed on that railing, waiting for the water to come, waiting to die. It's funny because I wasn't scared to die. The idea of it didn't terrify me or panic me or even make me nervous. I figured God knew when my time was, and if this was it, then this was it. I thought, "What a beautiful way to die—with the people I love the most." I had had so many blessings and met so many great people in my thirty-one years, and I could accept death if that's what was meant to be. I was upset that Debbie would lose all of us in one day, but I knew she was strong, and I knew I couldn't escape dying if it was my time. And yet—I didn't believe it was.

For some reason, despite the situation we were in, I just couldn't understand that there wasn't some way out for us. I guess maybe I thought if I truly let myself believe we were about to die, then it would happen. Or maybe it was my mind trying to shut out the emotions involved in facing death. Whatever the reason, I couldn't wrap my brain around actually dying, even though nothing about it frightened me. It was like half of me was at total peace with the idea of death and the other half of me was in total denial that it would happen. I knew from the look on my dad's face that he didn't have the same inner conflict that I did—he truly believed this was the end. Maybe the conflict is a natural reaction for some people in that situation. Maybe it's normal to hold out hope until the absolute end. It so difficult now to put into words the way it felt up on that railing—certain of both dying and living at the same time.

I was still hammering my dad with questions, in between telling everyone that I loved them. We also had his cell phone out, even though it didn't have international service, thinking that maybe by some miracle we could get a call out to Debbie to tell her good-bye and how much we loved her. We tried several other family members, just on the slight chance that one of the calls would go through. All I could think of were the people who had been in the towers or on that plane on 9/11, and how some of them had been able to talk to a loved one for one final time or leave a voicemail with a final good-bye. We knew we had to at least try, even if the odds were incredibly slim that it would work.

NO ONE CAN EVER REALLY KNOW HOW THEY WILL HANDLE THE IDEA OF DEATH UNTIL DEATH IS ACTUALLY STARING THEM DOWN.

One of the strangest things about that time on the railing was that none of us were crying. We're a pretty emotional family, me especially. I have yet to make it through one of those ASPCA commercials, with the heartbreaking dogs and cats, without bawling. I cry when I see cute babies. Everything makes me cry. So for me to not be emotional in that situation just baffles me. And Cindy, my amazing little sister, who has had to overcome her intense fear of flying, was being so astonishingly strong. She loves ships and being on the water and I knew that she had to be heartbroken over the irony of something this tragic happening on a ship when it had always seemed like such a safe place to her. But if she was scared or upset, she didn't show it. She was so strong and so brave throughout the entire ordeal.

Maybe we were all in shock, or maybe we were still in survival mode, but no one broke down, even at what we thought was the end. I know it had to be unbelievably hard for my parents to think of leaving Debbie, and I know they were both worried that something would happen and Cindy or I would die first and they would be forced to see it happen. But they stayed strong and just kept telling us how much they loved us.

I don't think there are many families out there that have faced death together and walked away. I'm sure there are some, but it can't be a normal occurrence. We were truly blessed that we had each other. We never fell apart or became hysterical or panicky. No one can ever really know how they will handle the idea of death until death is actually staring them down. I guess everyone hopes they'll be strong and dignified but secretly worries that they might break down. But we didn't break down. We banded together and spent what we thought were our last few minutes on earth talking about Debbie and other loved ones and how much we loved each other. While we might have lost a lot that night in terms of personal effects and our sense of security when we travel, no one can ever take away from us how we handled ourselves. I think it's a true testament to how much we all love each other that we were able to support one another at such a critical and life-altering time.

- -

CHAPTER:
THIRTEEN
NAME:
DEAN
DATE:
1/14/12, 12:00AM–12:20AM CET

- -

I had hoped that the stairwell would take us down a level so that we could get off the ship, but it was a dead end. One of the things I'd learned in the navy is that if a vessel is rolling over and you're on one of the open-air decks, you better figure out how to get off, and fast, because once it rolls all the way over, you're trapped. I had also recently seen a documentary about a World War I cruiser that had been hit by a torpedo from a German U-boat. It showed the ship starting to roll over and then suddenly you could see dozens of splashes in the water all around, where all of the remaining crew started leaping into the water to get off the capsizing ship. In a very short span of time, the ship sank. I knew if we couldn't get clear enough away from the ship before it rolled completely over, we wouldn't have a chance to survive.

So once I knew the stairwell wasn't an option, I thought to myself, "This is it." The girls told me later that my face at that moment said it all: I was waiting for death. I just knew the water was about to rush in and wipe us all out. I think we were in total shock, waiting for the end to come. I was hoping that it would happen all at one time. There's an old saying about how parents shouldn't bury their children, and I couldn't think of anything worse than if something happened and one of the girls went first. I wanted it all to be over with at once and all of us to go together and go quickly. Maybe something would even knock us out cold and we wouldn't know what had happened. Drowning is supposed to be a very painful death, so if we could avoid it somehow, we would be lucky.

We spent that time praying and talking. I knew that the last things we would see on this earth were each other and the people around us. Georgia had been holding a baby for a couple we had met on the lifeboat, but she handed her back so that they could spend their last few minutes with their daughter. But when the water didn't come, I thought, "What in the world is going on here?" Nothing was happening and it just did not make sense. What I didn't know was that the ship had come to rest on some rocks on the other side. I later learned we had drifted out to sea after our initial collision with the rocks, but a steady wind had blown us back to the shore so that when we rolled on our side, the rocky shore basically broke our fall. Some people might call that wind luck or fate, but our family knows it was divine intervention that saved our lives. We were so thankful for yet another miracle. The ship had come to rest at a little less than a ninety-degree angle, so for all practical purposes the ship decks were perpendicular to the water.

I could now hear helicopters in the air around us and I couldn't figure out what was going on out there. How could we possibly be floating on our side? It was sheer chaos down below us on the deck wall (now the floor) because I guess the other passengers had been waiting for the end like us and were equally confused when it didn't come. Once we realized we weren't about to die, I knew we needed to get back down to the wall since we had nowhere to go on the railing.

CHAPTER:

FOURTEEN

NAME:

GEORGIA

DATE:

1/14/12, 12:05AM–12:30AM CET

We all looked to Dean for help when our hopes of escaping down the stairwell were crushed. His expression was like nothing I had ever seen. His face said everything that words couldn't say. And at that point we knew that the ship was going down, that we were going down with it and there was no way to survive. It's like we were connected in such a way that we all just knew, without anyone having to say it out loud. I don't know if I could have told the girls what we were up against if they hadn't recognized it for themselves when they saw Dean's face. It would be so hard to tell your children that they are about to die. Never had I thought I would be faced with something like that, especially on a vacation cruise.

MY BIGGEST FEAR IN THAT MOMENT WAS THAT
WE WOULDN'T ALL DIE TOGETHER.

I was extremely proud of how brave and composed we all were in that moment, especially Cindy, the baby of the family. I knew how horribly frightened she can be when she has to get on an airplane and I knew she must have been crushed to think that the one place she felt the safest and happiest had just turned into her worst nightmare. What I realized then, and hope she realizes now, is how brave and strong she can be in the face of disaster.

One of the girls started a prayer and we all joined in. And then our thoughts and conversation turned to Debbie. We thought it was beyond sad that Debbie was going to lose all of us at once. We hoped she would know that we had all died together and that she wouldn't worry that anyone had been alone or scared. My thoughts went to my mom as well. What would she do without me when she had so little of her memory left, making the few constants she still had in her life so important? My mom had already suffered immeasurably years ago, when she lost my dad and my brother in a short period of time. Would she be able to handle another loss? Would she even understand what had happened to me? I worried too about my Aunt Bessie, whose care is also my responsibility. Who would make sure she was looked after if I wasn't there?

My biggest fear in that moment was that we wouldn't all die together. I didn't think I could handle seeing my children die. I asked Dean what he thought was about to happen and he told me the truth—what we all knew from his face—he thought this was it. And we all hoped and prayed that the end would come fast and no one would suffer or have to watch the others go first. I just kept praying, "God, make it go fast." I guess in some way, waiting on death is the ultimate equivalent of slowly removing a Band-Aid. And as a mother, I couldn't stand the thought of the whole process dragging out painfully for my children and my husband.

I had noticed that the young couple from Argentina with the little girl was on the railing next to us. The father was standing in front of me, holding his daughter. I'm not sure how much he had understood of our conversation, but for some reason he turned to me and said, "Take my baby." I instinctively grabbed the baby when he held her out, but then I had to hold the railing with my left arm and the baby with my right. She was really more like a toddler, so holding her wasn't that easy, and I'm not all that tall myself. The ship was still moving some (settling into place, we later learned) and I was worried I would drop the baby down the stairwell or to the deck below. I couldn't stand the thought of that happening with both of our families looking on. I thought we were most likely all about to die anyway, and the baby needed to die with her parents, not some stranger. She needed to feel loved and held by her parents, not confused. So I handed her back to them and told them, "Take your baby back. You need to be with your baby now."

To this day, I don't understand why they handed her to me. Maybe they thought somehow our family had a better chance of survival than they did. Maybe they thought that between the four of us, one of us would make it and could save the baby. Maybe they just didn't understand what was happening and handed her off in confusion. Maybe they thought they would panic and drop her. I don't know. People do strange things when they're under the stress of death. The one thing I did know was that she didn't belong with me when the end came; she belonged with the people who had brought her into this world.

So we huddled together and waited for the end—but nothing happened. We couldn't figure out what was going on and why we couldn't see the water yet. Valerie kept asking Dean why we weren't moving anymore. He told her he didn't know and couldn't understand what was going on because the water should have rushed in by then. Valerie really was our head cheerleader and she kept a clear and level head while enthusiastically encouraging all of us, each step of the way. It meant a lot to me to see my oldest daughter taking such a leadership role. We had all been so certain based on the ship's rolling that this was the end, and now it seemed we had been granted some kind of reprieve. We were still holding on to each other, but we finally decided that if nothing was going to happen, we needed to get down off the railing, away from the stairwell and find out what was going on. The only way down was to go back through the railing, but it was like getting down off the top of very tall monkey bars. We would have to jump through the space between the rails and drop down to the deck below.

Cindy came up with a plan right away and said she would go first to test it out, so she scooted through the railing and dropped to the deck. Once she was down on the wall, Valerie followed suit and dropped through. Then it was my turn. But as I was getting down between the rails, my life jacket got caught up on a small metal box on the railing. Gravity was pulling me down and my life jacket was keeping me up, choking me, with my head up at an awkward angle. I remember thinking to myself, "Oh my God, I am *not* going to die this way!" I had not gone through everything we had gone through (so far) to be choked to death by a life jacket hanging off a railing! So I grabbed the bottom of my life jacket and shoved it into my chest to pull it loose. Thankfully it worked and I slid through and down to the deck. Later I discovered I had pushed it up against myself so hard that it had left a bruise—a small price to pay to avoid the world's most ironic death. Dean said I was lucky I hadn't hit my chin on the railing and knocked myself out. But even that would have been better than being choked to death by a life jacket!

Once I had made it safely to the deck, Dean crawled over the rails and jumped down, and then we were all back together again. Technically, I guess we were on the wall. The chaos hadn't diminished, and the obstacles had increased because of the list of the boat. The wall we had to walk down had open doors and windows, and the upper part of the deck had giant gaps where the lifeboats had been. So even if we could figure out a way to get up there to the outermost railing, the walking would not be an easy task. I looked around at the chaos and the crazy position of the ship and thought if we survived, it would be a miracle and there would have to be some purpose to it all.

CHAPTER:

FIFTEEN

NAME:

DEAN

DATE:

1/14/12, 12:30AM–1:00AM CET

It took a minute for all of us to gather ourselves after the drop back down to the bulkhead. Once we made sure no one was hurt, we noticed a group of people gathering up ahead of us, towards the bow (or front) of the ship. We could hear lots of noise—yelling and general commotion—coming from the group and decided it was worth checking out, so we started off down the wall.

Walking down the bulkhead of a ship is harder than it sounds. Most of the doors were open so we really had to watch our step or someone could have fallen through. There were windows as well, and while they probably could have supported our weight, being designed to withstand storms at sea, we weren't chancing it, so we had to maneuver around those as well. It took us much longer to close the distance to the crowd, winding around obstacles this way, than it would have if we had just been walking down the deck of a normal, upright ship.

Luckily we still had enough light to see each other and see where we were going. Plus, we had used our own saliva to activate the lights on our life jackets. Normally, these little flashing emergency lights come on when they hit water—to help the rescue crews see where everyone is in the dark—so we licked our fingers and rubbed the moisture on the sensors to get the same effect. It was a very handy trick.

ONCE WE GOT CLOSER TO THE LADDER, WE COULD SEE WE WERE WALKING INTO TOTAL MAYHEM AGAIN. PEOPLE WERE PANICKED AND PUSHING AT EACH OTHER, MEN WERE SHOVING WOMEN AND CHILDREN ASIDE, OLDER PEOPLE WERE BEING TRAMPLED AS THEY TRIED TO CLIMB UP THE LADDER— IT WAS TOTAL CHAOS.

Once we got a little closer to the big crowd of people, we could see an extension ladder (the kind you might prop up against your house to climb up to the roof), rising out of the crowd towards the sky. Now this is kind of hard to envision, but basically, if the ship had been upright, the ladder would have been lying along the ground, stretching from one side of the deck to the other, and sticking out a little into one of the holes where a lifeboat had been. But since the ship was on its side, the ladder was leaning up against the deck, which was now the wall, with the last few rungs sticking up into the air where the deck ended.

To us, it seemed like this ladder came out of nowhere and we were excited beyond words. My guess is that the ladder had been used for maintenance and it had been left out on the deck. However it came to be there, though, it rose up ahead of us like a shiny, eighteen-to-twenty-foot miracle.

THERE WAS CLEARLY NO SUCH THING AS "WOMEN AND CHILDREN FIRST" IN THIS SITUATION. IT WAS EVERY MAN FOR HIMSELF.

Once we got closer to the ladder, we could see we were walking into total mayhem again. People were panicked and pushing at each other, men were shoving women and children aside, older people were being trampled as they tried to climb up the ladder—it was total chaos. This ladder was the only way to get off the deck and on to the side of the ship, and people were in a crazed frenzy to get up it. One guy was climbing up the backside of the ladder while an older heavyset woman tried to climb up the front. People were yelling at the guy, telling him to get off the ladder before he knocked it over. But he was desperate to get to the top, I guess terrified of what would happen if he didn't.

Maybe worse than him was the man climbing up the ladder and dragging his little girl with him by the strap on her life jacket. She couldn't have been more than five or six, if that, and rather than hold onto her around her waist or chest, he had gripped the strap loop on the life jacket right behind her head. She was hanging freely, flopping around like a rag doll, supported only by the belts and straps on the jacket. The top of it was up around her neck and was clearly making it difficult for her to breathe. Beside me, Georgia was yelling out, "She's choking! You're choking her!" I guess maybe he thought she was too young to climb, even with his help, and so this was the only way he could think of to carry her. Whatever his reasoning, it was appalling to watch, and the memory of that little girl flopping around still haunts me to this day.

There was clearly no such thing as "women and children first" in this situation. It was every man for himself. Valerie and Cindy couldn't stand watching the kids being shoved mercilessly out of the way, so within minutes of our approach to the ladder, they'd had enough. Valerie announced that she was going over there and was going to take charge. Valerie isn't normally the "take-charge" type, so for her to have had enough to take on a crowd like that really says a lot about how bad things were. She and Cindy muscled their way to the front and got as many of the children up the ladder as they could. They used themselves as a sort of shield to block all the desperate adults and started hoisting the kids up to safety. Once they had all the kids up, it was their turn to go. The girls turned to us, but before they could say anything, Georgia told them to get up the ladder and not to worry about us as we had lived our lives and wanted them to save themselves. We would get up the ladder if we could, but they needed to not waste any more time. I agreed with Georgia and told them to go on ahead. We told them that we'd be fine if we didn't get off the ship, but they needed to get up that ladder to whatever safety they could find.

The girls firmly and adamantly said "No!" We either all went or none of us went, but they weren't leaving us behind. Before Valerie and Cindy would go up that ladder, they said we had to promise to follow right behind them. In order to keep things moving, we agreed. They made us repeat the promise a few times before they believed us, but then they started up the ladder and once they got near the top, Georgia started up. It was still pretty crazy at the bottom of the ladder and I got separated at one point. I noticed there were a few more parents with kids coming up, as well as an older lady, so I let them start up ahead of me. It took the older lady a while to make it to the top. The girls yelled down at me to get up the ladder next, so as soon as a mom and her daughter got up, I started climbing.

I could hear Valerie yelling, "That's my dad! That's my dad!" I had no idea who she was talking to until I got near the top and saw a couple of German fellows who were helping people get off the ladder. As they helped pull me off, they told us we needed to head up and towards the front of the ship. The plan was to head to the highest point on the ship, in case it rolled more, or started sinking quickly.

As people got off the ladder, some were heading to the right (like us), up towards the bridge, and some went to the left, down towards the stern. The majority of the people headed left, to the back of the ship, where we later learned a rope ladder had been set up and was being used to get everyone down to the waiting life-boats. There are actually several pictures of this rescue operation that made their way around the Internet and news shows. But at the time, we didn't know what was going on towards the back of the ship, so we headed up and to the right, seeking the highest point we could possibly find.

Before we could make our way up the side of the ship, we had to climb through another metal railing, but the two German passengers went through first and then helped everyone else. As we started moving up the inclined outer side of the ship, I noticed these little pipes that were part of a sprinkler system, with little sprinkler heads attached, like you might see on the ceiling of a hotel room. The sprinkler pipes ran along the rows of windows and the water could be turned on to clean the windows off. Trying to make our way up the side of the ship was quite treacherous because it was slick, so what we did was hook our feet under the pipes for leverage. It made it more secure to climb because we weren't as worried about losing our footing and slipping.

Fortunately, we all had pretty sensible shoes on, since we hadn't gotten dressed up for dinner. I was wearing tennis shoes and the girls both had boots on, but regrettably Georgia had on flat shoes with no support. I couldn't imagine how it must be for all those women who had been wearing fancy shoes and were now barefoot. The temperature was easily in the forties and everything had a slickness to it, thanks to the ocean and the light mist. Unfortunately, Cindy only had a tank top on, and I started to worry she might be getting cold, especially now that we no longer had the protection of the ship around us, but were instead climbing up the side, out in the open, frigid air.

CHAPTER:

SIXTEEN

NAME:

VALERIE

DATE:

1/14/12, 12:40AM–1:00AM CET

The ladder felt like a miracle out of nowhere. I guess it had been a ladder used by the crew to paint or service the ship, but to us, it was so much more. It was a way out of this nightmare. Seeing the ladder made me feel like we had a chance—I knew we needed to get higher and this ladder was a huge opportunity. If we weren't going to be able to jump, we needed to get as high as we could.

The area around the base of the ladder was crowded with people yelling, screaming, and shoving. I remember there was a man going up the ladder with a child, pulling her by the life jacket instead of holding her. It was terrifying to watch and I was worried that the little girl wouldn't survive the climb because she would choke to death before her dad could make it up the ladder with her. It was incredibly disturbing to watch him drag her up the rungs like that. Life jackets aren't even that secure, especially on a child. She could have been seriously hurt. It was one of the worst things I have ever had to watch.

There were also a lot of older passengers who couldn't move very fast. They were shoving themselves in front of children to get up the ladder, but they were taking such a long time that it was stalling the entire process. My mom was especially frustrated by this. Sometimes people would start up the ladder only to be knocked down when someone behind them shoved them out of the way to take their place.

One elderly lady was slowly making her way up the ladder when, suddenly, a man (who I guess was too impatient to wait his turn) started climbing up the backside of the ladder. She almost fell when he got on the ladder and everyone on the ground panicked that he would knock the ladder over or possibly even break it and then no one would be able to get up to safety. There were so many people pushing others out of the way. It was really starting to upset me, especially because all of the children should have been the first ones up the ladder. I couldn't figure out what kind of human beings would push innocent children aside just to save themselves. It seemed so selfish, horrible, and cowardly. I think at that moment I was seeing the worst I've ever seen in human beings.

Next to me, a little girl had hidden her face up against her mother because the scene was so scary for her. That was the last straw for me—I just couldn't watch it anymore. This was way too much for me to endure and I decided we were going to get these children up that ladder, no matter what it took. So I took my four-foot, eleven-inch self and forced my way through the remaining crowd until I got to the base of the ladder. I had grabbed the mom with the little girl and pulled them through with me and once we got to the ladder, I gave them a push to get them headed up before someone could shove them aside again. There were a few other children around, and Cindy and I got them up the ladder next, blocking everyone else with our bodies so that they couldn't cut in ahead of the children.

Once all the children were gone, I turned to my parents. They tried to get Cindy and me to save ourselves and go without them, but we told them it was all of us together or none. Just like when Mom had mentioned us heading to Rome without them when Dad's blood pressure was up and we had refused, we refused once again. We weren't leaving them behind. I told them that I would go first so I could figure out what to do, but only if they promised to be right behind me. Once they promised, I started up the ladder. I remember going up as fast as I could, and about halfway up, I turned to make sure everyone was behind me. Cindy was directly beneath me and my mom was heading up behind her. My dad let a couple other people go in front of him before he started up.

I KNEW FROM TALKING TO MY DAD (AND WATCHING THE MOVIE *TITANIC*) THAT YOU SHOULDN'T JUMP OFF A SHIP UNTIL YOU ABSOLUTELY HAVE TO OR YOU COULD BE SERIOUSLY HURT, EITHER BY THE WATER WHEN YOU JUMP IN OR BY THE BOAT IF IT ROLLS OVER ONTO YOU.

When I got to the top of the ladder, I turned again to check on the others. They yelled for me to keep going but I needed to know they were all safe behind me first. At the top, a couple of men were helping everyone off the ladder. I told them if they helped me off, they had to help "my pretty sister and my mom and my dad." They were really nice, English-speaking German passengers and they promised to help get my whole family off the ladder. They pulled me off and up to the side of the ship. I pointed back down to Cindy and my mom and they helped them as well. Once Dad got up, they both pulled him off the ladder. Those men were extremely helpful and we spent a lot of our remaining "adventure" in their company. I will be forever grateful for what they did for us. At one point, I had thought they must work for the cruise line because they were doing so much to assist everyone else, but they were just very knowledgeable and helpful passengers. I felt kind of bad that I had insisted that they help my entire family, but I just wanted to make sure my family was safe.

I knew from talking to my dad (and watching the movie *Titanic*) that you shouldn't jump off a ship until you absolutely have to or you could be seriously hurt, either by the water when you jump in or by the boat if it rolls over onto you. So I figured we needed to stay on as long as possible and that meant going up to the highest point. The German passengers apparently agreed with me because they started guiding people up toward the highest part of the ship. We started climbing up the outside of the decks, and everything was angled and slick, so it certainly wasn't easy going. I was fortunate enough to be wearing my Ugg boots and I managed to wedge my feet under these little pipes that ran along the ship and were used to clean the windows. By using any railings we could find to grab on to and hooking our feet under the sprinkler pipes, we slowly but surely worked our way up.

There was a slight mist, which made everything damp and extra cold. I didn't notice it too much at the time because my adrenaline was still high, but I remember looking at Cindy in her spaghetti-strap tank top and thinking how cold she must be. I, at least, had my University of Southern California t-shirt on, and my boots were keeping my feet warm. As long as my feet are warm, I don't really notice a cold temperature that much, so I was very glad that I had hurriedly shoved my feet into warm boots when I was rushing out the door for dinner. At the time it had just seemed like the easiest thing to throw on with my t-shirt and yoga pants, considering I was still sleepy and we were in a hurry. Now it seemed like a miraculous stroke of luck or divine intervention that I had them on. I just hoped Cindy wasn't too cold and that we could find some way off the ship before it got any colder.

CHAPTER:

SEVENTEEN

NAME:

CINDY

DATE:

1/14/12, 1:00AM–2:00AM CET

"Pulling a Val" was starting to seem like a really bad idea. While wet hair and a lightweight tank top had been perfect for a quick dinner, now that I was on the side of a cruise ship in the middle of the night in January, it wasn't nearly as perfect. Thank goodness I had at least put jeans and boots on, or I would have been ten times more miserable. Plus, my life jacket helped give me some protection against the wind. But still, I was cold.

Climbing up the side of the ship was hard work. We had to maneuver around these random beams and other stuff that stuck out from the side of the ship, I guess where the lifeboats had been. It was hard to climb over them because we weren't completely flat so if you lost your footing, you could technically slide off. You had to hang on to something or someone for safety as you stepped around them. The German guys were helping us as we went along, too. They told us if we could get to the top, help should come. We could hear helicopters above us, so surely it wouldn't take long to get rescued, I thought.

As we got closer to the highest point we could reach, we

WHILE WET HAIR AND A LIGHTWEIGHT
TANK TOP HAD BEEN PERFECT FOR A QUICK
DINNER, NOW THAT I WAS ON THE SIDE OF A
CRUISE SHIP IN THE MIDDLE OF THE NIGHT
IN JANUARY, IT WASN'T NEARLY AS PERFECT.

noticed several other people were already sitting up there in a line, huddled against the cold. Once all of us had made it up, we turned and looked out. If I had to guess I'd say we were probably eight to ten stories high. It was dark, but there were lights from the boats and the helicopters, which I assume were all part of the rescue operation. We could see almost twenty boats surrounding us. We thought one of the helicopters was lifting someone off the bridge of the ship, not terribly far from where we were, but it was hard to see exactly what was going on.

We sat there, way up in the air, on the side of the cruise ship waiting to be rescued. But nothing happened. We could see that there were people on the other boats because they were lit up, but the boats stayed far enough away that if the ship flipped, they were out of her range. I couldn't figure out what they were doing there if they weren't going to help us. It was almost like they were just watching the spectacle.

I was really starting to feel the cold, but at least I still had enough adrenaline in my system to keep me from feeling the full extent of how frigid it was. Still, I was shivering. We were totally exposed and had nothing to block us from the wind and the mist. Plus we're from Southern California and spoiled by the beautiful weather, so anything below seventy degrees feels like freezing to us. And it was well below seventy—probably somewhere in the low forties. I was grateful for my life jacket because it was set up high enough to keep my neck and shoulders somewhat covered.

I remember talking to an Italian woman while we were sitting up there. I asked her what she thought we were going to do and when someone would come for us. But I quickly realized that she couldn't understand a word I said because she didn't speak any English. Basically, other than us, the only English-speaking people on the side of the ship were the German fellows and an Austrian guy. Conversation was limited.

We still had no idea that the ship had settled up against rocks. For all we knew, it could suddenly flip back the other way and we would have gone flying off the side and down to the dark, cold water below. And then the ship probably would have landed on us and crushed us (assuming the fall hadn't done us in first). So needless to say, it was a little scary sitting way up there in the air, on a ship we didn't know was stabilized, waiting for something to happen. The boat hadn't completely stopped moving, since it was still settling on its side and being moved a little by the waves. We just sat there, looking out and around, with no one helping us (or even trying to help us), hoping that the ship didn't flip again like it had earlier. Val was still asking Dad a billion questions—why weren't we moving, why did the boat seem stabilized, how were we going to get off the ship, were we still sinking—and Dad didn't have any answers. The whole situation didn't make sense to him either.

We didn't know how we could possibly get down to the water, and no one was making any effort to come to us, so we sat there and waited. Apparently, people were being rescued down a rope ladder at the other end of the ship, but we had no way to get down to them, even if we'd known we needed to. So we just huddled there in our little line, talking about what we should do. We must have sat there for about an hour. There were probably about fifteen of us up there, sitting and waiting. The worst part of being up that high was looking out at all the boats and knowing there were helicopters, but not seeing anyone making any attempt to rescue us. It was so frustrating. Most of the conversation during that hour centered on why all those boats were out there and no one was trying to help us. I wondered if they'd just leave us on the side of the ship forever.

Mom was really upset about the helicopters. We thought at least one man had been airlifted off the bridge, but after that, we hadn't seen another air rescue. She wanted to flag them down and try to get them to take us off. We tried waving our arms frantically and yelling to get their attention, but it didn't do any good. The worst part was being so close to being rescued, but feeling so far away because it seemed like no one was doing anything.

Finally, a few people thought they spotted a lifeboat close to the ship, with people getting on it, so the group started moving down slowly in a single-file line. I couldn't see all the way to the bottom to find out if or how people were getting off the ship, partly because it was dark and partly because those metal beams from where the lifeboats had been were sticking up in the air, blocking my view. We still didn't know how close to land we were, or whether there was a way from the ship onto the lifeboat, but we started making our way down the ship when it was our turn, hoping the lifeboat at the bottom would stay there long enough for us to all get off this floating nightmare.

CHAPTER:

EIGHTEEN

NAME:

DEAN

DATE:

1/14/12, 2:00AM–2:30AM CET

After about an hour of sitting way up high on the side of the ship, one of our fellow passengers decided that what we needed to do was make our way back down and towards the middle, where it looked like a lifeboat had gotten up close enough for people to jump on. He'd been up walking back and forth while most of us sat in our line, and he thought he'd figured out a way to get down there, if that lifeboat would stick around long enough. He seemed pretty excited about it, too. I remember noticing that he had on a dark jacket and dark pants, which looked kind of like a uniform to me, so I asked, "Are you a crew member?"

"Oh no," he said. "I'm an architect from Vienna." I should have figured he was another passenger because not once had we encountered a crew member taking charge of anything. But this passenger was stepping up and doing what needed to be done, just like the two German fellows had done at the top of the ladder and like Val and Cindy had done at the bottom of the ladder. I guess most of the crew members were either too busy following orders or too scared to step up or weren't even on the ship any more. Thank God for these assertive passengers we met.

The plan was that we would scoot down to an area a little ways below us, then crawl across one of the small strips between the big openings (where the lifeboats had been), make our way across to the middle of the ship, then use these thin ropes that hung down the side of the ship to guide us lower until we were close enough to jump into the lifeboat. Anything had to be better than sitting up there and waiting for a rescue that apparently wasn't coming, so we all decided to follow and hope for the best.

First, we'd have to climb back down the same way we'd climbed up, using the sprinkler pipes to anchor our feet. Most of that could be done in reverse, on our hands and knees. But the really tricky part would be maneuvering down the thin strips between the lifeboat holes. They might have been twelve inches wide and they were angled down, like the rest of the ship. There was nothing to hang on to either. To compound the issue, only about half of us spoke English, so it was difficult to get everyone on the same page.

Georgia told me later that she had looked at that small strip and thought there was no way she could get down it. But she quickly realized that if she wanted off the ship, she *had* to get down it. So she told herself that this was no time for saying "I can't," and that she *could* and *would* get down the side of that ship—no matter what.

Cindy said she'd go first down the twelve-inch strip to figure it out and then she could show us the best way to do it. Georgia followed behind Cindy, then Valerie went. I told them I'd wait until they were clear before I started, just in case I slipped. The girls are all pretty tiny, so I was worried that if I slipped, I might take one or all of them down with me.

Cindy led the way, scooting down on her butt, inching her way lower with her sister and Georgia behind her, following suit. Once they were on the far side, I started down, just like Cindy had done. Everyone cheered each other on as we made our way down that nerve-wracking, narrow part of the ship with giant openings on either side of us.

THE SMELL OF THAT CIGARETTE AS HE SAT THERE SMOKING WAS THE BEST THING SHE'D EVER SMELLED BECAUSE IT WAS JUST SOMETHING SO *NORMAL*. IT WAS THE FIRST *REAL* SENSORY THING IN A VERY *SURREAL* NIGHT. IT REMINDED HER OF PEOPLE STANDING AROUND OUTSIDE AFTER DINNER, SMOKING AND HAVING COFFEE OR A DRINK.

When we were all clear of the holes, we found another set of sprinkler pipes that we were able to use to scoot sideways until we got to the middle of the ship. Moving on our hands and knees was more painful than hooking our feet in the pipes. If anyone had slipped at that point, they would have gone sliding down the ship and taken a pretty sharp drop into the water. If someone came across a tricky area that needed special care, he or she would call out warnings to the others as we all made our way across the ship. After carefully crawling about halfway across the length of the ship, we finally found ourselves directly above the lifeboat and located the nearest rope that we could use as a guide to get us closer to the water and the lifeboat.

About this time we noticed the first member of the crew we had seen since being thrown off the lifeboat, sitting by the guide rope. I think he might have been from India and he spoke English really well. What amazed us most of all was that he was taking a smoke break. There he sat, on the side of the ship, at two-thirty in the morning, calmly smoking a cigarette while passengers were trying to evacuate this ship. Now none of us are smokers (although I used to be, a long time ago), and Georgia, especially, can't stand the smell of cigarette smoke. But she told me later that the smell of that cigarette as he sat there smoking was the best thing she'd ever smelled because it was just something so *normal*. It was the first *real* sensory thing in a very *surreal* night. It reminded her of people standing around outside after dinner, smoking and having coffee or a drink. It was such a mundane, ordinary act, and for her, the smell of it was incredibly calming.

The rope we used to guide us down the ship wasn't nearly sturdy enough to hang on to, but it was enough to keep us moving down in a straight line. The ropes were normally used as guidelines to help lower the lifeboats, but they worked equally well as guidelines for us to use to lower ourselves to the bottom of the ship. We'd switched back to sliding down on our butts again for this part. The girls were still ahead of me, and finally we all made it to what was basically the bottom of the ship. It was easy to tell when we were nearing the bottom because the color of the ship changed from white to dark red. At the bottom, we could easily see the lifeboat in the water just below and in front of us. Now all we had to do was get on it and we were home free—we thought.

CHAPTER:

NINETEEN

NAME:

CINDY

DATE:

1/14/12, 2:00AM–2:30AM CET

Making our way down the ship was much harder than going up had been. Thankfully, the Austrian guy was really good about directing us and finding the easiest and safest ways to go. We were able to walk down the first little bit, but then we had to alternate between hands and knees and scooting on our butts. We used the sprinkler system pipes again to hook our feet into as we walked, then crawled, down to the boat deck level. I seriously don't know what we would have done without that sprinkler system.

We spent most of the trip down in a single-file line. In fact, when we had to maneuver between the two gaps where the life-boats had been, there wasn't another option other than single file. We had such a narrow space to move down, that it was barely wide enough for one person. It was kind of like if you took a house that had two really big windows with a one-foot panel separating them, turned the house at an angle on its side, removed the glass so that the windows were just big holes, then tried scooting on your butt down the foot-wide panel, without falling into the window holes on either side. Not an easy feat under the best circumstances, then factor in the cold, wet, and windy weather. And if one person had slipped, anyone (or everyone) ahead of them could have been knocked down, too. We were potential human dominoes once again.

At the bottom of the thin panel, we had to watch out for the large metal beams that stuck out, where the lifeboats had once been suspended over the water. Once we got past those though, we had another handy set of sprinkler pipes to hook our toes under as we crawled sideways towards the back of the ship, away from the bridge area where we had been. We had to make it to the center of the ship, above the lifeboat before we could start the final descent down. Going down and sideways at the same time would have been too risky. When we got to the middle, directly above the lifeboat, we used this lightweight rope as a guide while we scooted the rest of the way down on our behinds. The rope was flimsy and useless for safety, so if anyone had slipped, grabbing onto it probably wouldn't have done much good. We just had to go slowly, like we were sliding down a steep and slippery hill.

Out of the four of us, I had gone first for most of the journey down the side. I wanted to figure out the best and safest way and be able to let the others know. Several people were ahead of me though, including the Austrian, so I was able to have a guide too. The Austrian guy was great about sending back tips as to the safest, fastest or simplest way to navigate a certain part or a difficult section. We all worked together really well. I don't know if the people who didn't speak English were able to benefit from the tips as much, but at least they could watch him and try to imitate the way he went.

It's so weird now when I look at pictures of the ship, still on its side, to think that we were on that—that we climbed *down* it.

It's crazy. Never in a million years would I have thought that any of us would be capable of anything like that. And now, waiting for us at the bottom of the ship, was our shot at rescue—finally.

CHAPTER:

TWENTY

NAME:

VALERIE

DATE:

1/14/12, 2:30AM–2:45AM CET

One of the things that stuck out the most to me about that night was the pain. The side of a ship is not a very forgiving surface and all I could think of as we moved along was how bad my knees hurt—and how I'd never been so happy to feel pain as I was at that moment. I think the reason it felt good to be in pain was because it meant I felt *something*. I was alive—and so close to being rescued from this living nightmare.

Cindy led the way down the ship as we navigated between large gaping holes and inched our way slowly towards safety. She was balanced and went slowly and carefully and we all followed her lead. My mom was right behind her, and I followed my mom, with Dad bringing up the rear. None of us were exactly dressed for the occasion, and going down the side was slippery and treacherous, so slow and steady definitely won the race. It took a lot of concentration, so cheering each other on and calling out warnings was basically all the talking we made time for.

As we were making our way down to the lifeboat, I had thought we would have to jump in the water and swim out to the boats, once we got to the bottom. I didn't realize until we got much closer that a boat was waiting right there for us. We had gotten to the red part of the ship (the part that's supposed to be underwater) and I could look out and see one of the lifeboats that had been launched earlier, banging up against the bottom. It wasn't tied up to anything, so I guess they had just pulled it up as close as they could get it for all of us to jump in. I imagine keeping it as close as possible wasn't an easy task, since the water currents kept changing rapidly, probably due to the weather and/or the waves made by rescue boats.

EVERY PART OF THIS NIGHT, INCLUDING THE RESCUE, WAS FRAUGHT WITH DANGERS.

I could tell right away that jumping in wasn't going to be a simple task. You not only had to time your leap, based on how the boat was moving, but you had to jump out and down in order to get through the opening in the enclosed lifeboat. It would have been nice to just walk onto the lifeboat, but they couldn't exactly set up a little dock for us, so we had to take our chances with one final test of our physical and emotional abilities. I'm not sure whether it was the wind or because we were in a rocky area of the sea, but the water was pretty rough, and I remember hearing the noise of the lifeboat slamming into the ship over and over, and thinking, "I hope the lifeboat doesn't sink too." That was all we needed.

Cindy was the first to jump onto the lifeboat and because the angle was so tough to maneuver, she aimed for the roof of the lifeboat. The water was just too choppy at that moment to try to jump into the opening on the side of the boat. Mom went next, and also wound up on the roof. Another woman followed their lead and jumped to the top as well, but she was still very distraught and shaky once she got up there. Mom and Cindy tried to help calm her down while a guy who was up on the roof with them (and who had been directing people in their leaps off the ship) took off his jacket and draped it around Cindy. It was such a sweet and selfless gesture to witness, and I thought about how situations like this usually bring out either the best or the worst in people. Men like him restored my faith in humanity after seeing so much of the worst side of people back at the ladder.

THERE WAS AN ALMOST CREEPY, LONELY QUALITY TO IT—A SHIP THAT WAS SUPPOSED TO BE THE BEGINNING OF THE MOST AMAZING VACATION OF MY LIFE, NOW JUST LAY THERE ABANDONED ON ITS SIDE.

Once it was my turn, I was told to jump into the boat, instead of on top of it. I was so excited to be getting off that ship, but it was a little daunting to face that jump. It had to be at least fifteen to twenty feet, out and down, into a hole roughly the size of a set of open double doors—and it was a moving target. I was really hoping I wouldn't break my legs jumping down, although I wouldn't have minded if that's what it took to get me safely to land. With all the circumstances I had endured that evening, I needed my legs in order to save myself or others from another disaster because, by that point in the night, nothing seemed impossible.

So I steadied myself and took a few deeps breaths to calm down and jumped for it. I felt the impact of the landing in my already sore legs, but I was once again happy to be able to *feel* because it meant I had made it! After I was safely in, I turned to watch my dad jump. The two German guys, the Indian crew member (who we later learned was a photographer on the ship), and the Austrian guy were the last ones still on the ship, and they were helping people time their jumps. Dad was next, but as soon as he got ready to leap, the lifeboat suddenly lurched away from the ship thanks to a wave, and the men reached out to help my dad catch himself. If he hadn't been able to stop his forward motion, he would have landed in the water between the ship and the lifeboat. And if the boat had been slammed back up against the ship again, he would have been crushed between the two. It was just one more reminder that every part of this night, including the rescue, was fraught with dangers.

Once my dad had gotten back in position and the lifeboat was back up near the ship, he attempted the jump again, and this time the waves cooperated. Finally, we were all safely on board the lifeboat—as safe as people who've just escaped a shipwreck can be on a boat. Mom and Cindy were content to make the ride to shore on the roof, but they were told that they had to jump from the roof into the lifeboat or we would not be able to head to shore.

I remember the Austrian man finally getting on the boat and donning a construction hat, much to our surprise; then he handed out emergency water to all of us. I'm not sure where he found the construction hat, but somehow it perfectly suited him. He seemed like such a hero to me, and he made sure to keep checking on everyone, even when we were all safely on the lifeboat. The water he gave us was in little plastic bags and had probably been in the boat for quite some time, but despite the slightly salty taste to it, it was the best water I had ever had.

It was eerie to look back up at the ship. We were literally the last few people off the ship that night. It was about 2:45 a.m. and this whole ordeal had started around 9:45 p.m.—five hours of anguish had elapsed since we had been a happy but tired family, sitting down to our first dinner on the *Costa Concordia*. Over four thousand people had been on the ship at that time. And now it was deserted. It was so huge and so quiet as we looked up at it from our lifeboat. There was an almost creepy, lonely quality to it—a ship that was supposed to be the beginning of the most amazing vacation of my life, now just lay there abandoned on its side. The whole night almost didn't seem real.

I think, looking back, that we must have all been on a serious adrenaline rush that night. My mom isn't a very athletic person, yet she was able to jump up to that railing, jump back down, climb a good-sized ladder, crawl to the highest part of the ship, crawl and scoot back down to the lowest part of the ship, and make a giant leap onto the roof of a lifeboat. I know if I had asked her that morning if she thought she could do any of that, she would have laughed and said "No way!" But she did it. We all did it. And we were finally on a lifeboat—one that would actually take us to land—and we assumed our nightmare was coming to an end.

You would think by then we would have known better than to assume things like that.

PART TWO:

SURVIVING ON SHORE

CHAPTER:

TWENTY-ONE

NAME:

DEAN

DATE:

1/14/12, 2:45AM–3:00AM CET

We hadn't been on the lifeboat but a few minutes when I heard the Austrian passenger, who was sitting next to me, cry out, "Oh my God! Look at that hole! There's a rock still in there!" I turned to follow his gaze just as we were passing by this massive gash in the red part (the area below the waterline) of the ship. "Rock" was the understatement of the year because the piece that was jutting out must have been at least the size of a military tank. The spotlights from the helicopters were bright enough that we had a clear view of the damage that had caused our night and vacation to take such a horrible turn for the worse.

There were bags of emergency water on the lifeboat and Valerie said it tasted better to her than any name brand bottled water ever had, even though it had a stale, salty taste to it. She had been asking me questions most of the night, a lot of them about why we hadn't sunk and how the ship seemed to be floating on her side. I had been as frustrated as she was because none of it made any sense to me either and I had no real answers for her. But our questions were about to be answered.

As we rounded the ship, we suddenly learned a little piece of information that answered all the questions Valerie had asked that I hadn't known the answer to—namely, that we were only a short distance from land and had apparently run aground. In fact, we were so close to land that we were pulling up to the dock within ten minutes of getting on the lifeboat. I was totally shocked that we weren't in the middle of the sea. I turned to look back at the shadowy ship, now resting on its side up against an underwater rocky ledge, and I thought, "What in the world was a ship this size doing that close to the shoreline?" It blatantly didn't belong there. I couldn't, for the life of me, figure out why we would have been cruising so close to land on such a massive cruise ship. The *Costa Concordia* is large even by today's cruising standards. In fact, it was one of the largest cruise ships we had ever been on, and we've been on a lot of cruise ships. So why wasn't it out in much deeper water?

From the lifeboat, it looked like we were pulling into a quaint small village. We didn't know at the time that Giglio is actually an island. We wouldn't learn that for several hours, when we were made to get on another boat in order to reach the mainland of Italy. Before we got off the lifeboat though, we were able to get a decent view of the entire ship from the docks (thanks to the spotlights shining on it). It looked like a kid's toy boat that had been discarded in a too-shallow kiddie pool, except much, much larger. It was then that I realized we had spent five hours crawling all over that ship and finally jumped to a lifeboat to be rescued and yet (other than from the mist) none of us had even gotten wet!

On our short trip to shore, Georgia spotted a lighthouse. I think we knew then what it must have felt like, years ago, for sailors who had spent weeks or months at sea, when they first caught sight of one of those night beacons that meant dry land was near. To make it even more poignant, our priest always calls the Orthodox cathedral that we attend a "lighthouse on rocky shores" because our church is in a difficult area of Los Angeles. So to suddenly see an actual lighthouse on an actual rocky shore, in the midst of such a difficult time, was very moving for us.

> I ALSO SAW SEVERAL BLACK BODY BAGS THAT OBVIOUSLY WEREN'T EMPTY. THIS HARD EVIDENCE OF CASUALTIES MADE IT ALL THE MORE CLEAR TO ME JUST HOW LUCKY WE WERE TO BE WALKING OFF OF A LIFEBOAT. APPARENTLY OTHERS HADN'T BEEN SO LUCKY.

Giglio isn't a large island and it has maybe fifteen hundred people living on it. It's located in the Tyrrhenian Sea (which is part of the larger Mediterranean), off the coast of Tuscany. It's known mainly for its rocky coast—making it even more puzzling that we had been sailing so close to it that we actually ran aground. It made about as much sense to me as steaming full speed ahead into a section of the North Atlantic known for its icebergs must have made to the survivors of the *Titanic*. It's that moment when you realize that other people's stupid decisions can change your whole life—and not in a good way.

Our lifeboat pulled up to a tiny little dock and we all unloaded amid the chaos that was taking place on land. The more than four thousand passengers and crew that evacuated the *Costa*

Concordia and took refuge on that tiny island must have seemed like a full-scale invasion to the citizens that lived there. There were almost three times as many people on the ship as there were people who called that island home. Despite a heroic effort on their part, they just couldn't accommodate as many people as were suddenly flooding their shores. Emergency personnel were running around trying to deal with the cold and injured people. Lights and sirens from emergency vehicles were flashing and blaring. Several thousand people were milling around. So far, rescue wasn't any less chaotic than danger had been.

I imagine the people on that island did the best they could when four thousand people suddenly came barging ashore in the middle of the night. But there was no way that they could be expected to be prepared to deal with the madness that came in trying to take care of all of those cold and miserable passengers and crew. I also saw several black body bags that obviously weren't empty. This hard evidence of casualties made it all the more clear to me just how lucky we were to be walking off of a lifeboat. Apparently others hadn't been so lucky.

CHAPTER:

TWENTY-TWO

NAME:

GEORGIA

DATE:

1/14/12, 3:00AM-6:00AM CET

Our family was among the last people to be rescued off the ship and brought to land, so the emergency supplies were basically all gone. We could see other people with emergency blankets wrapped around them and a line where people were waiting and hoping to get one of the few remaining blankets. I was really getting worried about Cindy who had been shivering for over an hour now. It was starting to rain in earnest and she had been cold for so long. We all had felt the cold of the night, but Cindy had it the worst since she only had on that tank top. After five hours of this madness, I had learned that no one was going to look after my family but me, and if we wanted or needed anything, standing around and patiently waiting wasn't going to get us anywhere. So at that moment, I made a "mom" decision and went up and just grabbed one of the shiny blankets from the small stack left and immediately wrapped it around Cindy. I couldn't have handled it if Cindy had gotten ill from exposure after everything we had already been through. I somehow managed to grab an extra one too, so we wrapped both around

Cindy and all huddled together for added warmth.

It was then that we slowly started to process what had happened to us. It was also then that Valerie looked at me with wide eyes and said, "Mom, do you know what day it is?" I wasn't sure what she was talking about, so I told her I didn't.

"It's Friday the thirteenth," she said. "And it's eleven years ago today that Uncle Jimmy died."

MY PARENTS HAD STARTED OUR FAMILY'S LOVE OF CRUISING. EVERY YEAR, THEY TOOK THEIR GRANDCHILDREN ON A CRUISE AS THEIR GIFT BECAUSE THEY WANTED THE KIDS TO HAVE THOSE MEMORIES WITH THEIR GRANDPARENTS WHILE THEY WERE ALIVE, RATHER THAN LEAVING THEM AN IMPERSONAL INHERITANCE WHEN THEY WERE GONE.

And that was it for me—I lost it. After five hours of not shedding a tear or even getting choked up, when she reminded me of the anniversary of my brother's death, I started crying, and for several minutes, I just couldn't stop. It hadn't occurred to me what day it was; I usually try not to remember death anniversaries, and instead remember what the person's birthday had been. But thinking of how we had lost Jimmy to colon cancer eleven years ago and how close Debbie had come to losing the four of us on the exact same day was just too much for me. How would she have coped with that? It was devastating to even think about.

WE LEARNED MUCH LATER THAT TWO OF THE PASSENGERS WHO DIED WERE AN OLDER COUPLE WHO HAD BEEN ON THEIR VERY FIRST CRUISE TOGETHER.

We all immediately thought that maybe Jimmy, who had cruised with us several times, had been our guardian angel that night, looking out for us as we miraculously came through so many obstacles. Dean commented on how many close calls we'd had and how likely he thought it was that we'd had some unseen help. The girls were convinced that we had made it through so much because we had Uncle Jimmy looking out for us.

Thinking of my brother then reminded me of my parents. My parents had started our family's love of cruising. Every year, they took their grandchildren on a cruise as their gift because they wanted the kids to have those memories with their grandparents while they were alive, rather than leaving them an impersonal inheritance when they were gone. It's because of them that cruising had become such an integral part of our family time together. But when I tried to picture my parents on that ship with us (as they had been on so many of our early cruises), the idea of them navigating all of those obstacles we had faced in order to get to safety was an impossible one—I couldn't see them being physically capable of managing it. In fact, despite being the avid cruisers that they were, neither of my parents ever learned how to swim! I knew that they would never have been able to survive what we had gone through. Just noticing the black body bags that were being wheeled by us on gurneys made me wonder how many of them had been older people who had been cruising for years and had now had their lives snuffed out by the thing that had previously brought them such joy. We learned much later that two of the passengers who died were an older couple who had been on their very first cruise together. They had never even had a chance to enjoy cruising as we had for so long.

I was honestly relieved that my dad had already passed and that my mom really didn't understand things anymore because it would have caused them both so much hurt to know that cruising—the activity they had given to us, which had bonded us all together—had turned into such a disaster. That thought made me realize how close I had come to leaving my mom in such a fragile state and leaving Debbie in a position of being responsible for her along with everything else that goes with losing loved ones. My aunt also relies on me and she had traveled with us many times herself. I couldn't wrap my mind around what she and Debbie would have felt if they lost us on a cruise.

We spent most of our time huddled up with our blankets, talking about all of these feelings that we were all having. The reality had definitely started to sink in for us, and we were relieved to think that our family back home wasn't aware of what we had been through. It never occurred to us that this shipwreck was considered major news. We had more pressing matters to consider.

When I had run into our cabin to get the life jackets, I had grabbed my purse, thinking that I might need Dean's blood pressure medicine later. But climbing around on walls and jumping up to (and back down from) a railing and climbing a ladder (and the side of a ship) had required both hands, so at some point in the evening, I had been forced to let the purse go. (Technically, I think I had gotten frustrated with trying to hang on to it while dealing with all those obstacles and had thrown it against a wall.) Now I was worried about Dean again and I knew we needed to get medication for him, just in case. We started asking around and learned that there was a pharmacy open in the small village— we still didn't know it was an island—so we made our way there, hoping they would speak enough English to understand what we needed.

Unfortunately, no one at the pharmacy spoke any English, but by writing down the name of the medication and utilizing a few good hand motions, we were able to communicate what it was we needed. The people who owned that pharmacy were among the nicest that we met during the entire ordeal. Not only did they take Dean's blood pressure for us, but they got online to look up the medication we had named for them, to figure out what the equivalent was in Italian. Then after they had filled the prescription for us, they refused to take payment for it when Dean got out his wallet. They had opened their pharmacy in the middle of the night so that they could help the people who had been brought ashore, and I guess they didn't want anyone thinking they were trying to take advantage of the situation, so they weren't charging people for medications. Honestly, they were some of the sweetest and most generous people I had ever met in my travels.

Once Dean had taken his blood pressure medicine, we turned to other important matters—finding food and finding a restroom. There was a little café that had opened up and we heard they had coffee and pastries and a "little girls'" room, so we headed that way. It was a tiny little café and there were about a hundred people all crammed in there. You literally couldn't move around. I'm not claustrophobic but I felt smothered inside the café and feared that people would get trampled to death. I saw the urgency of leaving as soon as we could get what we needed. Again, being the last ones off the ship meant that there wasn't much left by way of food, so Dean headed over and bought up what little was left and got everyone some hot drinks to warm us up. It was lucky that we had his wallet still because the café owners apparently didn't mind if people thought they were taking advantage of the situation—they were charging for food and drinks. We were just grateful that they were open, but I wondered what we would have done if Dean hadn't taken a nap with his wallet still in his pocket. I guess we would have gone hungry for a while longer.

HE SAID THAT THE CAPTAIN AND A LOT OF THE OTHERS "PARTIED REALLY HARD" AND SOMEONE MUST HAVE DONE SOMETHING WRONG AT SOME POINT IN THE NIGHT TO CAUSE US TO RUN AGROUND. THAT WAS MY FIRST HINT THAT HUMAN ERROR HAD BEEN THE CAUSE OF OUR DISASTROUS EVENING

Once we had all visited the restroom and gotten our pastries and drinks, we headed back outside to avoid being trampled in the crowded café. There was a small table right up against the wall, so we stopped there to enjoy our assorted pastries. I had a chocolate-filled croissant, which (at least to me) was the best thing I had ever tasted. I can still remember how good it was, as it all but melted in my mouth. Of course, it's possible I would have felt the same way about stale bread after everything we had been through!

There was a lot going on, in and around that small café. It seemed to double as a bar because we noticed when we got our food that it also served alcohol, and several people had already taken advantage of that fact and starting drinking, probably to self-medicate and numb the memories of that tragic night. We also heard a lot of crying and saw one woman who was completely hysterical. We eventually learned that she had lost her husband on the ship. We looked at each other and just couldn't fathom what it would be like if one of us hadn't made it. It was unreal to even think about that and our hearts went out to that poor lady. The amount of dazed people along with their personal emotions crammed in to that tiny little café was something none of us will ever forget.

While we were standing around eating our pastries and drinking our nice warm drinks, we struck up a conversation with a couple of crew members. On all of our previous cruises, we had enjoyed getting to know the crew members as they would always share the inside scoop on what was happening aboard the vessel. On that night, I remember asking them specifically what had happened. I was still shook up over the whole situation and I thought maybe they could shed some light on it. Several of the men were photographers (our Indian friend from the side of the ship was also there—the one who made me feel better just by smoking a cigarette) and one of the men told us that the wreck didn't really surprise him. He said that the captain and a lot of the others "partied really hard" and someone must have done something wrong at some point in the night to cause us to run aground. That was my first hint that human error had been the cause of our disastrous evening. Up until then, I hadn't questioned the "why" or the reason behind it all. I had been too busy just trying to survive to care why we were in that position in the first place. But now it made me angry, thinking that other people's recklessness had been the cause of so much tragedy. Apparently one of their fellow photographers was assumed to be among the dead because he had been trapped on a lower level, the last they had seen him. It seemed everywhere we turned was more shocking and tragic news.

One of the crewmen mentioned that he had talked to his family already because they had seen what happened on CNN and had been worried about him. This was the first time we realized that what had happened to us was major news around the world! I panicked once I heard that because I didn't want our family back home to see what had happened, hear there were casualties, and not know whether we had survived or not. He informed us that, according to his family, CNN was reporting that there were three people injured, but nothing else. Well, we knew from seeing body bags that there were more than three people who hadn't survived, let alone all those who had been injured. Obviously the news stations didn't have the latest information or were choosing not to release it. I was relieved though, because it meant our family wouldn't be as worried.

Most likely that's why news stations don't report back on the full extent of tragedies like that until people have a little time to contact family members. They probably don't want to cause panic among people at home when they can't contact their loved ones and don't know whether they survived or not. Since we were on the side of a newsworthy, catastrophic event, it made me grateful for responsible journalists.

After talking to the crew members, we decided to head to the church where we had learned that people were taking shelter from the cold and rain. It was a beautiful church and was situated so as to be the main focal point of the small island village. It was also the largest building on the island. Once again, being the last ones off the ship meant we were also the last to try to find shelter. The church was already completely packed full of people and we couldn't even get inside. We headed back down to the café in the cold rain where we rejoined a Canadian mother and her adult daughter whom we had met immediately after coming ashore. Meeting any fellow English-speakers was comforting, and we quickly made friends with the two women. Aside from being fellow English-speakers, we also learned that the daughter was a social worker, which struck home with us since that's Debbie's chosen field as well.

With the church being closed, we had no idea where to go or what to do. No one was giving out any instructions and there was no overall organization by any Costa representatives. Any help that was given was given by the people of the island out of the goodness of their hearts. (Many of them had brought out their own sheets and blankets for the wet and cold passengers to wrap up in.) We saw a ferry being loaded, but we had no idea where it was going. We considered trying to get on it and just take our chances. We could also see buses and walked over to try to get on one. When the door opened though, we learned that it, too, was full. But when it drove off, we watched it circle around for a while and come back to where it had started, with all the same people still on it. Apparently they were just using the buses as another way to keep people warm and dry—they weren't actually taking them anywhere because there was nowhere to go.

So we set off to find any kind of shelter—an alcove, an awning, anything that would keep us warm. Finally, we discovered a toy store that had opened up. Inside, it was mainly crew members sitting around on the floor, but we did run into our German friends who had been with us on the side of the ship. The son of the family that owned the store had heard about the wreck and gotten up in the middle of the night to open the doors so that people could take shelter. They also had a restroom and were letting people use that as well. We met a pregnant lady in line for the restroom and told her to cut in front of us since I was willing to bet she needed to use it more than we did! I've had three kids—I remember what it was like being that pregnant. Although I can't imagine what it must have been like to escape a sinking ship while pregnant!

We found a spot to sit together on the floor (our life jackets made convenient cushions to sit on), and it was so nice to finally be inside someplace warm. Our clothes were wet and we were still cold, but at least we were out of the rain and could start warming up. The rest of the family that owned the toy store came in and handed out chocolate candy to all of us. When the father arrived, he brought several articles of clothing with him and handed them out to some of the wet, cold people on the floor. The girls were given nice warm sweatshirts to wear. The shop owners really just opened their hearts and their business to us and we were so grateful.

There was no place to stretch out, so we were sitting up against the wall. I was starting to get upset because it seemed like, even though we were finally on land, things weren't any better organized than they had been on the ship. Now, instead of being stuck on a sinking ship, it seemed we were stranded in a small Italian village. I was really beginning to despair that things were never going to get better, when I looked up and noticed three little ceramic dolphins on a shelf on the other side of the store. Dolphins have always been kind of like a good luck charm for me and seeing them at that moment brought me a sudden sense of peace. As many cruises as we've been on, I've always loved to look over the side of the ship and see dolphins swimming along beside us. For as long as I can remember, they've had a calming effect on me. Seeing those little toy dolphins made me think that, despite everything we had been through and the helplessness we now felt, we would eventually come out all right.

CHAPTER:

TWENTY-THREE

NAME:

DEBBIE

DATE:

1/13/12, 9:45PM–10:15PM EST

I was bothered the rest of that evening by the same nagging feeling. I just couldn't shake it and I could not figure out why I still hadn't heard from my family. My friend was as bothered by it as I was; she thought it was really unusual for my family to not attempt to contact me, especially after I had emailed them my concerns. I tried to tell myself that they were just tired and jetlagged and that there was no reason to worry.

I only had my mom's and Val's email addresses saved on my phone so I couldn't email anyone but them—in this world of smartphones, I don't memorize much anymore. I had only emailed my mom earlier, figuring she would be the one to check email before anyone else, but so far, I hadn't heard anything. I had traveled with them so many times before that I had a good idea of what their schedule would have been like that first day. My sisters would have gone to take a nap right after lunch. I knew Mom would have wanted to unpack right away and Dad may have rested for a while, but he doesn't usually nap. He likes to get his body used to the new time zone as fast as possible.

Normally, he helps unpack and then maybe watches a little television. It was easy for me to track their activities that day since I had vacationed with them so often before. I knew at some point after lunch, Mom probably would have set up the Internet, and I *thought* she would have emailed me right before or after dinner, so I was frustrated because I still hadn't heard from her.

By now, I was sitting at a late dinner with my friend and her family. I just couldn't shake this bad feeling so I left my phone out on the table, which is something I normally wouldn't do, especially when eating with people I had just met. I was sure they were going to call or email me very soon, so I didn't want to miss my chance to talk with them and make sure they made it safely to Rome and to see how Dad was feeling. Sure enough, not long into dinner, my phone rang. It wasn't a number I knew, so I was hoping it was my mom, calling from the ship. I got up and excused myself from the table, but when I got outside and answered, it wasn't Mom, just a family friend. At first, I was annoyed that I had left dinner to take the call, so I figured I would keep the call short. But I quickly learned the purpose of his call was to ask if I had heard about the cruise ship accident off the coast of Italy.

He was one of the few people who were aware that my family had taken a cruise in that area right after my wedding. He had heard about what happened and was calling me to see if I knew anything about it and if it was their ship. I've been on many cruises and several of them have involved "incidents," so I wasn't immediately concerned. I figured it wasn't anything major and told him it was probably a small fire or something and not a big deal. But then he said that he wasn't trying to upset me (he is a psychologist by profession), but that the news was reporting at least one casualty—a sixty-five-year-old man—and I might want to make sure it wasn't their ship.

HE TOLD ME THE ACCIDENT HAD HAPPENED
ON A SHIP FROM THE COSTA CRUISE
LINE. . . .I ASKED IF HE HAD CHECKED
BOTH OF THE CRUISES THEY WERE TAKING,
AND HE SAID HE'D FLIP THROUGH AND LOOK
FOR THE NAME OF THE OTHER ONE.
THEN—DEAD SILENCE ON THE LINE.

At that point, I started to get a little anxious and had to remind myself to stay composed and positive as there were other people standing outside the restaurant too. My dad was sixty-four at the time, and it was a little too close for comfort to hear of a man around that age being reported dead. Still, I thought, what were the chances that it was even their ship? I tried not to worry too much about it and told him thanks for the heads-up and that I would check it out.

I have been on a few cruises where there had been incidents that were unusual, but I figured that just comes with being on a large ship with many different people. When I was a teenager we were on a cruise where another teenager died of alcohol poisoning, and there was another cruise where the ship felt like it was about to roll over, it had tilted so much (my sister and I had actually gone flying from one side of the room to the other, the list had happened so fast). I had also been on cruises with minor fires, where no one was hurt, and on a few where people had to be airlifted off the ship due to illness. I knew things could happen on cruise lines, and I knew sometimes people had even died while cruising, but I didn't want to assume anything terrible had happened to their ship at this point. Being on a cruise ship always seemed relatively safe to me—I couldn't fathom a catastrophic tragedy happening on a cruise ship, especially in this day and age.

My bad feeling had never gone away, though, and I still hadn't heard from anyone in the family, so I figured I'd better check this story out. Luckily, before I had left on my trip, I made sure that Jonathan had a copy of my parents' itinerary. I also brought a copy with me. Normally, I would not put that as a priority before a trip, but with all of us heading in different directions, I thought a little extra planning wouldn't hurt. Since I didn't have my copy of their itinerary on me at dinner, I called Jonathan to have him check. I thought if he could look up the itinerary really quickly to make sure that it wasn't their cruise then I would be able to rejoin the dinner party and not have any worries. I asked Jonathan to get on the Internet and find out what had happened and what the cruise ship's name was, then compare that information with the family's itinerary. I told him where I had left his copy so he could check what ship the family was on.

He agreed with me that it was probably nothing and was very calm and mellow while he pulled up the information. Once he found it, he told me the accident had happened on a ship from the Costa cruise line. I remembered that one of their cruises was on the MSC cruise line, but I didn't know what the other one was. I didn't remember hearing the name Costa, but I had him check anyway. He looked and said that I was right—they were taking an MSC cruise. I asked if he had checked both of the cruises they were taking, and he said he'd flip through and look for the name of the other one. Then—dead silence on the line.

When Jonathan didn't immediately respond after checking the name of the second cruise line, I started asking, "What is it? What is it?" He told me to stay calm and then said, "It is their ship." I almost dropped the phone, and said, "Oh, my God, their ship sank!" Calm was not an option for me at that point—I was hysterical. My thoughts immediately flashed to the sixty five-year-old man who had died. What if that was my dad? So there I was, outside of the restaurant, crying, yelling about a ship sinking, while people stared at me. Thank goodness my husband is a veteran of the U.S. Air Force and very calm in situations like this, because he immediately took over thinking so that I didn't have to. This gave me time to take it all in and gain quick control of my emotions. His first thought was that we both needed a plan.

Jonathan told me to go back to my hotel and book a flight home immediately. He was going to call the State Department and Mom's cousin and find out what was going on. I don't know what I would have done without my new husband at that moment. He had only been married to me for one week and he already had so much to endure. All I had to do was get back to LA and we would handle the rest together. I told him to call me back with any information he uncovered, then I hung up, headed back inside, walked up to the table with my friend and her family, and informed them bluntly, "Their ship sank."

- -

CHAPTER:

TWENTY-FOUR

NAME:

DEBBIE

DATE:

1/13/12, 10:15PM–1/14/12 4:00AM EST

- -

Of course, shocking news like that is bound to generate some confusion and strange reactions. My friend looked at me funny and asked, "What are you talking about, Debbie?"

"My parents," I said. "The ship they're on—it sank. People are dead."

My friend immediately jumped up and said we were leaving. While we drove hurriedly back to the hotel, I called my mom's cousin—I wanted to talk to someone in the family. Once we got back to our hotel room, my friend took over dealing with the airlines and booked us a flight back to California for the next day. Her husband—also a veteran of the US military—got on the phone, trying to get as much information as he could about what had happened. By now, we had heard that the ship was off the coast of Giglio, an island in Italy. My friend's mom speaks some Italian, so she tried calling the authorities on the island to find out anything she could from them.

Between our tablets, smartphones, and CNN, we were frantically searching for any information we could find about what had happened. My friend, my mom's cousin, my husband, my friend's family, and I were calling anyone and everyone we could think of that might give us information—the cruise line, the State Department, the U.S. embassy in Rome. But it seemed as if no one had any information that they were willing to provide us. We heard the same thing from all of them—no one knew anything. I remember asking someone if the Red Cross was going out to help, and I was told that there weren't enough people involved so the Red Cross would not go out. That didn't seem right to me since I've seen the Red Cross respond to much smaller disasters than a large cruise ship sinking.

By this time, we were watching CNN's coverage of the disaster from our hotel room. I didn't understand why no one I was calling could give me any information when clearly there was plenty of information to be had by the news stations. I knew the information about the Red Cross couldn't be right, and we couldn't get through to the authorities on the island. I'm not sure where the holdup in information was, but it seemed that no one knew anything about survivors, casualties, or injuries. I was still completely in the dark about what had happened to my family.

THE ONE TIME IN MY LIFE THAT I NEEDED TO GET OVERSEAS AND THERE I WAS WITHOUT A VALID PASSPORT. I WAS SICKENED BY THE THOUGHT THAT IF SOMETHING HAD HAPPENED TO MY FAMILY, I COULDN'T EVEN GET OVER THERE TO CLAIM THEIR BODIES.

It seemed like everyone I talked to had this nonchalant attitude about my questions, and they had trouble showing compassion for what I was going through. I was getting really discouraged that the people who were supposed to be able to give me information and assistance were instead giving me nothing and making me feel like I was imposing on their time by being worried about my family. It was a shock to me because I guess I had always believed and hoped that there would be people to assist you and provide you with the information that is needed in a time of disaster and distress. Apparently that isn't always the case.

After getting nowhere on the phone, I figured that instead of flying home to LA, I would get on a flight to Rome so that I could find out what was going on at the source and be there for my family. At the time, it seemed like a rational plan—until I realized I hadn't renewed my passport. I have probably had a valid passport since I was ten, but with all the wedding planning and everything else going on, I had let it expire in December, thinking I had plenty of time to renew it before Jonathan and I left for our European honeymoon in May. The one time in my life that I *needed* to get overseas and there I was without a valid passport. I was sickened by the thought that if something had happened to my family, I couldn't even get over there to claim their bodies. My panic was escalating.

The news stations were reporting more confirmed deaths by now and we could clearly see the giant cruise ship, lying on its side in the water off the coast of the Italian island. I knew that the death toll wasn't all in, and the news was not saying how many, if any, of the casualties were Americans. All I could think about was the sixty-five-year-old man, and I started to worry that something had happened to some of my family while the others had been left to watch them die. It's probably not rational thinking, but when you're in that situation—not knowing what has happened to loved ones—your mind goes in a million different (and equally horrible) directions at once. You're trying so hard to think only positive thoughts and stay optimistic, but your brain can only focus on all the "what ifs" that *might* have happened.

My mind was in overdrive. What if only my sisters had died? What if my sisters were okay but my parents had died? What if they had gotten separated and couldn't find each other again? I was "what-iffing" myself to death. Needless to say, I didn't sleep at all that night. I told my friend to get some rest because we were going to need to be up in a few hours to drive to the airport for our flight home, but I couldn't do anything other than watch coverage of the wreck on television and pray. I was fluctuating back and forth between thinking about how strong my family was and how I just *knew* that they could survive anything, and thinking about the reported casualties and how bad it looked with the ship lying that way in the water. I was distraught!

Anyone who has ever had to wait to find out the fate of a loved one knows what that night felt like to me. I can only imagine how military families feel every time they hear about war casualties affecting whatever branch in which their family members are serving. And I know now that families of the *Titanic* passengers had actually stormed the offices of the White Star Line trying to get updated survivor lists the instant they were released, as they spent three excruciating days waiting for the remaining passengers to arrive safely in New York. I now have an idea how they must have felt. If I could have stormed the offices of Costa that night, I would have.

I think I might have been able to keep my thoughts optimistic if I hadn't already been so worried about my dad and then heard that a man about his age had died. That was just too close for me. And I was worried that if something had happened to my dad, how would the others have coped? Would they have been able to get through it and save themselves? We are such a close family, and losing any one person would be devastating to the rest of us. I was trying to stay positive but I wanted and needed to be braced for the worst possible scenario. Maybe if I didn't know any specifics about the casualties, I wouldn't have been as upset.

Rationally, I knew that Mom, Dad, Cindy, and Val were all experienced cruisers. I knew that they had done dozens of muster drills and were well-informed about how to board a lifeboat. I knew that my dad had naval experience and was no stranger to being on large ships in stressful situations. I knew that everyone in my family could swim, and I knew that they were all strong people and would fight hard to survive. But I also knew that my dad's blood pressure had been up and that a man about his age was dead. Those two facts were enough to override the rational part of my brain and make me think the worst. And nothing anyone could say to me could force the rational part to take back contol.

CHAPTER:

TWENTY-FIVE

NAME:

GEORGIA

DATE:

1/14/12, 6:00AM–9:00AM CET

We stayed in that toy store until dawn. We were still sitting with the Canadian mom and daughter and, between the six of us, we were rotating out shifts to check the ferries to see if we could all get on one (by now we knew that we were on an island). The ferries were being used to shuttle the emergency vehicles back and forth to the mainland, so there was never much room left for passengers—and they had over four thousand people that they had to get off the island. Getting on a ferry was no easy task. We weren't going to push our way on when we knew that there were still many injured people who needed to get to the mainland faster than we did. But we were seeing the same desperate panic in people forcing their way onto the ferries as we had seen on the ship with people trying to get onto lifeboats. We didn't want to make things worse than they already were, and at least we had someplace warm and dry to wait.

Our German friends were also taking turns checking the ferries with us. One of them came in a little after the sun started coming up and told us that there was room on the ferries for all of us. Before I left the toy store, though, I went to the owners and asked them to write down their address so that I could send them something when I got home to thank them for their kindness and generosity in letting us camp out on their floor. A lot of people had left the store hurriedly and it was fairly trashed inside, so our family stayed around for a few minutes extra to help pick up some of the garbage left behind by others. I didn't want to leave them with such a mess after everything they had done for us. I wanted that family to know how much we had all appreciated their hospitality.

When we got to the docks, there was a large ferry that everyone was trying to push their way onto, and next to it was a smaller boat (I think it was some kind of water taxi) that was also being used to shuttle people to the mainland. We decided it would be safer to take the smaller boat. While we were waiting, I noticed divers, still in their gear and wetsuits, around the dock. I guess the recovery mission had already been going on for the better part of the night because the divers looked extremely exhausted.

As we were getting ready to board the boat, we noticed the first Costa representative that we had seen all night on the dock at a table, asking all of us for our identification, specifically our cabin cards, which are the main forms of ID used on cruise ships. It was shocking to me that she never inquired if we were all right or if we needed anything. Most people had gotten off the ship with only the clothes on their backs, so I'm not sure what good the company thought it was going to do to ask us for identification. Dean was already irritated at the total lack of help that had been given by the company, so before she could ask us for anything, he asked her, "Where have you guys been all night?"

She didn't respond to his question, but instead asked us for our cabin cards. Dean was the only one of us who had anything on him because he still had his wallet, but he didn't have his cabin card, just his California driver's license. He told her that, and she said he was the first person she had encountered that had *any* form of ID (and yet she continued wasting time and resources by asking everyone). The girls and I had nothing to show who we were, and when we told her that, she said she at least needed to get our names so that she could "keep count of people."

That really annoyed me. Keep count of people? They hadn't bothered to keep count of us when we were left on the ship to fend for ourselves. They hadn't bothered to keep count of us when we had landed on the island and been given *nothing* and left (again) to fend for ourselves. But *now*? Now they wanted to keep count of us? I just looked at her and wasn't going to take any more of her lack of empathy and said, "I'm out of here," and we pushed past her onto the boat.

Getting on another boat wasn't something we were looking forward to, but at least this boat had heaters, and the warmth was much appreciated since our clothes were still wet from the night before (or really only a few hours before). We found a table at which to sit and were given some water. I remember feeling stunned and exhausted by the whole night and it was still very surreal to think of everything we had been through. We still couldn't figure out where the authorities were or any of the rescue organizations that we're so used to seeing in the United States. We understood that the people on the island weren't equipped to deal with all of us (although they went above and beyond trying), but we had thought that by now the cruising line would have put something more organized together than just a few random representatives hounding people for their cabin cards.

From the window of the water taxi, we got our first daytime view of the *Costa Concordia*, lying on her side in the water. It was very painful to see this horrific sight. We had seen the gash and most of the ship the night before as we went past her in our lifeboat, but looking out and seeing the whole thing like that, with the sun streaming down on her, was unbelievable. Dean pulled out his BlackBerry and took a few pictures. We had already started to notice how sore we all were from our miraculous ordeal and had found bruises, scratches, and cuts that we didn't necessarily remember getting, but looking out at that ship (from which we had somehow escaped) shed a little light on the way we felt physically, to say nothing of how we felt emotionally.

AFTER EVERYTHING WE HAD BEEN THROUGH ON THE SHIP, HEARING ANYTHING STRANGE ON A BOAT WAS ALMOST ENOUGH TO SEND THE WHOLE GROUP OF US DIVING OVER THE SIDE.

The running suit I had been wearing all night was still really wet, and my shoes and lower pant legs were covered in mud. I tried to dry them as much as I could on the boat ride over. Just getting out of those wet shoes for a few minutes and warming my feet by the heater felt so comforting. We were all hoping that dry clothes waited for us once we got to the mainland. We were never told on the boat where they were taking us or what was to happen. We just got on this boat and hoped for the best. Surely there would be a more thorough rescue operation somewhere.

The girls and I were a little nervous about being on the boat, but Dean told us not to worry because we could easily jump into the water and swim if something happened, since this was a much smaller boat. That helped a little—knowing we had some control over our fate. There had been no one to ask, other than the one representative, and she was too busy getting names and IDs to answer any of our questions. I'm not even sure she was aware of where people were being taken.

The water taxi we were on had these buoy-like balls along the sides, just above the windows, which acted like bumpers when the boats were up against each other. As we were sitting there at our table, heading away from Giglio, I had put my head down on the table out of sheer exhaustion. Suddenly, one of those balls came loose and slammed into the window right next to where we were sitting! Everyone on the boat jumped a foot out of their seats. After everything we had been through on the ship, hearing anything strange on a boat was almost enough to send the whole group of us diving over the side. People were panic-stricken, asking what had happened. Was something wrong with this boat too? Could we possibly have luck *that* bad? We quickly figured out what was causing the noise, but it didn't do much to alleviate anyone's worries, and we all continued to jump a little every time it slammed into the window. Our nerves were just too frayed to handle anything else at that point.

Finally, we pulled into the docks at St. Stefano on the mainland of Italy. As we got off the boat, we immediately noticed a heavy military presence. They had set up a triage unit for the injured as well as barricades to help organize the massive amount of reporters that were standing around. It was a huge production, and it wasn't the most organized I'd ever seen, but at least it was something, and that made me hopeful. Unfortunately, my hopefulness was short-lived. Cindy was the first to walk off the boat and she was immediately stopped by a member of the Italian military and asked to hand over her life jacket. Apparently they were taking up life jackets and using them to get a count of the people rescued off the ship—at least that's what we were told.

Cindy had been the coldest of all four of us, and for the better part of the night, especially high up on the side of the ship, that life jacket had been her only real protection from the wind and the cold. The jacket had become an icon of survival for her. She tried to tell the officer that she wanted to keep it and needed it to be warm (and really, to feel protected), but apparently he really needed that life jacket. She was already shaking and nervous and upset, but when he actually ripped that life jacket off of her, it was almost more than she or I could handle. It was so demoralizing for her and very upsetting to me. I was next in line, but I had my running suit jacket over my life jacket, so I figured I could hide mine under the jacket and get past the military officer. Then, when we were out of his view, I would give mine to Cindy. I wanted her to feel safe and protected again. Unfortunately, the officer caught me trying to smuggle the life jacket past him and he was pretty rude when he called me out on it. I immediately handed it over, realizing that we had better not mess with these people. The last thing we needed was to be tossed in an Italian jail and left there for God knows how long.

Our family was in a foreign country, only one of us had any ID, none of us had our passports, and we were basically at the mercy of the Italian government. It definitely behooved us to cooperate, so we all handed over our life jackets. As we walked away from the docks, the shock of everything, compounded with the loss of her protective life jacket, was overwhelming for Cindy and she collapsed, crying. The media was already shoving cameras in our faces and it was just too much for her. She was immediately taken to the triage unit and given hot tea to help warm her up. They gave the rest of us hot tea and cookies as well, and then wrapped a wool army-style blanket around Cindy, for which we were grateful. They offered to get Cindy to a doctor, but she didn't want to get in an ambulance and be taken to a foreign hospital, so as soon as she felt up to it, we headed back out of the triage tent.

SO THERE WE WERE AT THE SCHOOL; THERE WAS NOTHING LEFT TO EAT AND WE WEREN'T ALLOWED TO USE THE PHONES. IT WAS BEWILDERING. AFTER EVERYTHING WE HAD BEEN THROUGH, I HONESTLY JUST STOOD THERE, BEYOND MAD, BEYOND DISTRAUGHT, JUST BEWILDERED. AT WHAT POINT WOULD THIS RIDICULOUS NIGHTMARE END?

Nearby, they were loading up school buses to take us some-where, but again, we weren't told where—just that we needed to get on a bus. As Cindy was getting on, they noticed that she still had a wool blanket wrapped around her, and apparently the blanket had to be returned to triage, so once again she was forced to give up something that was keeping her warm and making her feel protected. It broke my heart to see the look on her face when she had to part with first the life jacket and now the blanket. But there was nothing I could do to stop them. It was just too risky and we needed to keep moving.

Once we were all without blankets and on the bus, we were taken to a school in St. Stefano. Since several of us are educators, going to a school was fairly comforting, especially for me as I have been an elementary principal and always considered school my second home. All of us have happy emotional associations with schools. To make things even better, as we got off the bus to head into the school, we were told that we would be given a meal inside and allowed to make a phone call. Well, of course, that was the best news we had heard in a while. Finally, we could call home.

But as our luck would have it, by the time we walked into the school, all that was left was juice. We could handle the lack of food though, because in a room off to one side we could see a large table with rows of telephones on it. When we got to the table, a Costa representative asked to see our personnel card. I informed her that we were not crew members; we were passengers and just wanted to call home and let them know that we were okay. We really thought they would make an exception for us, but that's when she told us that the phones were not for us, they were for Costa personnel only—and then proceeded to have us escorted out of the room. We were devastated and couldn't understand why we were being treated this way.

So there we were at the school; there was nothing left to eat and we weren't allowed to use the phones. It was bewildering. After everything we had been through, I honestly just stood there, beyond mad, beyond distraught, just bewildered. At what point would this ridiculous nightmare end? There were police around, but no one was telling us where to go next or what to do. We had been dropped at this school in the middle of a town we had never been to and it appeared that once again, we had to fend for ourselves.

Finally though, our luck changed, and a reporter with the

Associated Press noticed us standing around and came over to ask if we spoke English and if we were Americans. When we told her that we did and we were, she asked if she could talk to us about what had happened on the cruise ship. We didn't have anything else to do, so we figured why not, and said sure. She introduced herself as Nicole and asked if we knew where we were going or what we were supposed to do. We told her that we had no idea where we were going or what we were supposed to be doing, because we had yet to receive any useful instructions. She must have immediately sensed our frustration because she got us some chairs so that we could all sit down in a quiet corner for an interview.

I asked Nicole later why she had chosen us for an interview. She was an American correspondent in Rome and spoke several languages very well, including Italian of course. She said she realized early on that this was a news story with the potential to make history and she wanted to interview someone who spoke her native English so that she could make certain that she was getting the story across as accurately as possible. There were only about five hundred people total on the ship who spoke English and were either from the U.S., England, Australia, or Canada, but she had seen us standing there, looking lost, and decided to see if we'd be willing to talk to her. After we had answered all her questions, she asked us what we needed and we told her we wanted to get to the American embassy, but we didn't have a phone to contact them. Nicole very nicely called them for us and let us use her phone to talk to them. I told the contact at the embassy that we needed to get our emergency passports and get home, and they told us to get to Rome as quickly as possible so that they could help us. The last thing they told me was, "We are closing soon but we will wait for you to come." We had no idea that the embassy had hours of operation, so we were definitely grateful that they stayed open for us!

After we handed her phone back to her, Nicole gave us her card in case we needed to get back in touch with her, then helped us find the correct bus that would take us to Rome. She was really the first person who helped us get started in the right direction. If someone had asked me before that day who I thought would be the most helpful after a disaster such as that one, I would have never dreamed the answer would be a member of the press—the authorities, maybe, or the company responsible for the accident, but certainly not a reporter. And yet, that's who finally stepped up and helped us—an AP reporter named Nicole. And she did it *after* we told her our story, so we knew she wasn't helping us just to get our cooperation for a story. She just did it because it was the right thing to do. I'd never been so grateful for the media as I was at that moment.

CHAPTER:

TWENTY-SIX

NAME:

CINDY

DATE:

1/14/12, LATE MORNING– LATE AFTERNOON CET

Talking to Nicole was such a relief for us. Without her, I'm not sure we would have known where to go or what to do. We didn't even know how far from Rome we were, so we had to ask Nicole. She said we were about two hours away, which was surprising for me because I guess I had assumed we were closer than that once we got to the mainland. Apparently not—we still had a ways to go before we were even near our embassy.

We told Nicole good-bye and boarded the bus to Rome. There was no way to get seats all together so Dad and I sat toward the back and Mom and Val sat toward the front. My dad and I figured we would try to get some sleep on the long ride. All roads may lead to Rome, but they definitely aren't all smooth and flat. We had just gone up a bumpy hill and we were coming down the other side when all of a sudden, we heard and felt this rumbling sound coming from under the bus. I guess the bus was just downshifting to come down the hill, but the last time we had heard weird noises like that was on the ship when it ran up against the rocks, so obviously we were a little freaked out. Dad and I just looked at each other with this eerie sense of déjà vu—it was almost exactly like the shuddering vibrations and scraping, creaking sounds we had heard on the ship, and it really scared me that something was going to happen to the bus. We were literally only about twelve hours removed from when everything went south on the ship, so anything that even *remotely* reminded me of that initial feeling was unnerving.

MANY OF THE REST OF THEM WERE STRAIGHT-UP RUDE ABOUT EVERYTHING—VAL SAID IT FELT LIKE WE WERE BEING TREATED AS IF WE HAD SUNK THE SHIP, LIKE IT WAS SOMEHOW OUR FAULT.

I managed to sleep a little bit on the bus ride to Rome, but it wasn't very restful. I'd doze off for a short while and when I would wake up, I'd think maybe it was all some horrible nightmare. I would get my hopes up—and then I would realize that it wasn't just a nightmare and we were really on a bus to Rome, without our passports or any of our belongings. It was like waking up the morning after someone has died and forgetting for a minute that you've lost that person. Then when you remember, it all comes flooding back and you have to feel the hurt all over again. Every time I woke up from one of those little naps, I had to relive the shock that we had really just been on a shipwreck, had jumped onto a lifeboat, and spent the night on the floor of a toy store. It was a surreal shock, every single time.

Dad and I didn't know it at the time, but Mom and Val were sitting next to two other Americans, from New York, and they had a phone with international service. At some point on the drive, they were nice enough to let my mom make a short phone call home to let the family know that we were all okay. They thought Debbie was still in Miami and didn't know whether she would have her phone on her, so they called my mom's cousin (Val's godmother) at her house, figuring she'd be the one most likely to be home and answer. Mom told her that we were all okay and safe and asked her if she could get in touch with Debbie and tell her to please get back to LA so that she could meet us there when we finally got home. (We didn't know that Debbie was already trying to get back.) It was only a fifteen-second call, but Mom said later that it felt really good to know that we had finally made contact with our family back home.

When we got into Rome, we were taken directly to the Hilton Garden Inn at the airport. Mom had tried to get them to just take us straight to the embassy so we could get our passports, but the Costa representative on the bus said we had to go to the hotel first. Once we got to the hotel, our primary concern was to call Debbie. Luckily we were given a room and told that we could use the phone as much as we needed to. I was so relieved because I wanted to talk to my sister so badly, and finally I could.

We left a message for Debbie because her phone was off. We later found out she was on a plane to LA. Back in the hotel lobby, we found several representatives from the cruise line and told them that we needed to get to the American embassy so that we could get our passports, but they told us we couldn't leave the hotel. I was confused—so first we were told we had to go to the hotel and now we were being told we weren't allowed to leave it?

Several people told us that there was going to be a meeting around 1:30 that afternoon and we had to be there for it. We were also told that the other embassies were sending representatives to the hotel and that we should tell ours to do the same. By now we had noticed that there were very few Americans at our hotel. My mom thought they had possibly split us up on purpose. Luckily, we still had our Canadian friends with us.

Costa fed us "lunch" that consisted of bananas and juice and some kind of pasta. Everyone was mostly milling around but we found a few seats in the bar area where we could sit down and eat. Our plan was to wait around downstairs near the lobby for the meeting. Also, the television was on in the bar, so we could watch news coverage of the wreck, finally. To our shock, we saw the ship's captain being arrested. We still didn't know what had caused the wreck, other than the gossip we had heard from the photographers who said that the captain partied a lot. We were starting to think maybe there was some truth to that, if the authorities were already arresting him.

The all-important 1:30 came and went and no meeting happened. No one bothered to tell us why we didn't have a meeting—we just didn't. I was getting really frustrated with the whole situation and was trying to get another rep to help us by explaining the situation. Maybe she was just trying to be nice, but when she told me she "knew what we were going through," that was the last straw for me. I told her (in no uncertain terms) that no, she did *not* know what we were going through because she had *not* been on that ship for five hours and she was *not* stranded in a foreign country without her passport. She was at *work* in her *home* country and had no idea what we had gone through and no right to even assume that she could understand.

Sadly though, she was one of the nicest (albeit incredibly

misguided) representatives at the hotel. Many of the rest of them were straight-up rude about everything—Val said it felt like we were being treated as if we had sunk the ship, like it was somehow our fault. I guess maybe we were a massive inconvenience for them, in their eyes.

There were a few medical personnel at the hotel who were examining the passengers at Costa's request and we decided it might be worth having Dad's blood pressure checked out. Plus, Mom's wrist was hurting and we figured it couldn't hurt for all of us to get checked. They took Dad's blood pressure for him and I think it was around 140/100—which is pretty high—but we were told that it was "no problem" and he was "perfectly fine." After hearing that, Dad told us he wouldn't trust them to take care of a dog, let alone check any of the rest of us out, so we left without getting any further medical attention. They wanted us to sign a release saying that we had been examined and were fine (probably so that we couldn't hold them responsible later), but Mom said, "No way."

The Costa representatives still weren't being very helpful. On the bus, one representative had told my mom that they had our passports waiting for us at the hotel—the passports that they had taken from us when we got on the ship. But once we were at the hotel, no one ever mentioned giving them back to us. We had hoped it would happen at the mysterious 1:30 meeting, but when the meeting didn't even happen, we lost most of the remaining faith we had in the company. All we wanted was transportation to the embassy, but they kept telling us we couldn't leave. We finally got the number for the American embassy so that we could call them and explain the situation and hope that they would send someone to us.

Unfortunately, calling the embassy wasn't much help either. They sounded really sympathetic and told us they would definitely help us get our passports and get home—just as soon as we came down there to them. We explained that we were basically being held hostage by the Costa representatives at the Hilton and that they wouldn't let us leave, but they kept telling us we had to come down there in person. They wouldn't send someone to us. Mom told them that all the other embassies had sent people to the hotel; but it didn't matter. They just kept repeating that they were waiting for us there—we *had* to go to them.

My mom finally gave up trying to convince the embassy to send someone to us and we decided to try one more time to convince the hotel to let us leave. When we talked to one of the Costa reps again though, we were told (again) that we could not leave. Our embassy *had* to come to us. We absolutely could *not* leave the hotel. So Mom called the embassy back and told them (again) that we still weren't allowed to leave. The embassy informed her that Costa could not keep us at the hotel. But this time, instead of making us fight (and lose) the same battle all over again, the woman at the embassy said that she would call the hotel and talk to someone for us. Now we had some hope. Unfortunately, she called one of the other Hiltons in Rome and was told that they didn't have a record of us there and that they weren't holding anyone at that hotel. We tried once more with the Costa representatives and were told one final time that they could not let us leave.

We knew we really needed to get to the embassy because clearly they weren't coming to us and Dad's blood pressure wasn't in good shape, so we tried talking to the police that were at the hotel, instead of the Costa personnel. The police seemed understanding and said they would talk to the hotel about letting us go. (By this time, there was press everywhere, so I guess the police were there to keep everything controlled.) But when they asked the hotel personnel if we could leave to get to our embassy, they were told the same thing we had been told—we had to stay there until our embassy came to us.

This was quickly becoming more ridiculous than anything we had already experienced in the past twenty-four hours, and that's saying a lot. One more time, Mom tried the embassy. We didn't know this at the time, but by now, the American embassy knew who we were thanks to multiple phones calls from our family at home and the State Department. The embassy told Mom that the situation was ridiculous (which we knew) and that we had to get down there; Costa couldn't hold us hostage. I don't know what we expected, but I had always assumed that the embassy would do anything to help an American stranded in a foreign country. Apparently that's not entirely the case. While Mom was on the phone with the embassy that last time, the Canadian mom and daughter came in our room, crying. We asked what was wrong—apparently they had asked the Costa reps for the number to the Canadian embassy, but no one would give it to them. And we thought we had it bad. They couldn't even *contact* their embassy; they didn't even know where in Rome it was. Mom was still on the line with our embassy so she asked them about the Canadian embassy and learned that it was right down the street from ours. If we could all get to the U.S. embassy together, they would point the Canadians in the right direction to get to theirs. But first, we had to get out of that hotel.

Earlier in the afternoon, we had tried to get the hotel to call a cab for us and were told about some alleged taxi strike. Now, all six of us were in our hotel room trying to figure out a way out of the hotel so that we could find a cab driver willing to cross the picket lines. Dad said he'd bet that there were willing cabs at the airport. That was when Val came up with a plan.

CHAPTER:
TWENTY-SEVEN
NAME:
VALERIE
DATE:
1/14/12, LATE AFTERNOON CET

I was shocked at the way we had been treated since arriving at the hotel. It wasn't the hotel staff that was the problem, it was the Costa representatives. They were treating us like we had done something to wrong them. We had been given a meager lunch of bananas and juice. We had been told lies about a meeting that never happened and the location of our passports. Now we were being held against our will at the hotel. It seemed as though they were annoyed at us for what happened—like we had somehow blown a hole in the side of their ship and caused it to sink.

In fact, ever since we had gotten off that ship, we had been treated poorly, with the exception of the pharmacists, the owners of the toy store, and the AP reporter, Nicole. We were given blankets and they were taken away. The food was sparse and at times nonexistent for us (although I am grateful that they at least gave us something). We were denied the use of phones because we weren't Costa personnel. This was all after we had managed to escape from their ship without any help from them. It was unbelievable.

IN A WEIRD WAY, THIS EXPERIENCE GAVE ME
A DEEPER APPRECIATION OF WHAT IT MEANS
TO ME TO STEP UP AND HELP OTHERS WHEN
SITUATIONS CALL FOR IT.

Maybe as Americans, we were so used to the type of disaster-relief efforts that we see in our country, that we didn't realize it doesn't work that way in other countries. I'm sure there are people who endured Hurricane Katrina and her aftermath who might argue that it doesn't always work all that well in our country either. But I feel like for the most part, Americans go out of their way to help people who survive horrific events. From earthquakes to bombings to tornadoes to explosions, American people and businesses make collective efforts and pull together to help out the survivors with food, shelter, clothing, and emotional support.

We weren't in America though. We had barely been fed, we were still in the same clothes we had been wearing on the ship at dinner, and we were being held captive at our hotel. It felt like the struggle to get off the ship had only been the beginning of our plight. Our bigger struggle was to find our way home from this nightmare. Honestly, most of the Italians that we met in Giglio and those that worked at the hotel, including the police that we talked to, were very nice and tried to be helpful, but there was only so much they could do. Costa was clearly calling the shots and no one was prepared to confront them head-on in order to help us get home. The Costa personnel at the hotel were being downright nasty to us at times. I hate to use that word, but that's sadly the way they were acting.

In a weird way, this experience gave me a deeper appreciation of what it means to me to step up and help others when situations call for it. My life has always been centered on volunteering and doing for others. I had gone on this trip hoping to connect more with my Mediterranean roots, but instead, I was finding myself more and more grateful for my family-oriented upbringing, which emphasized giving assistance to others in times of tragedy. Despite the fact the Costa representatives were acting the way they were, I have such an appreciation for the way the Italians in Giglio stood up and did what was right for all the people affected by this tragedy. I will always be grateful for their big hearts and kindness.

But kindness wasn't going to help us get home. We needed to find a way out of the hotel and to the embassy without getting caught. Then, at that very moment, it was like a huge light bulb lit up in my head. I had a good intuitive feeling and needed to act on it. I had been in the elevator earlier and seen a notice about a complimentary shuttle service to the airport, about fifteen minutes away. When my dad pointed out that there were probably plenty of cabs at the airport, it all fell into place—if we could somehow get on a complimentary shuttle to the airport, we could find a cab and get to the embassy from there! And even if we couldn't find a cab because of the strike, airports are a mecca of transportation. Surely we could find a bus or train or some other form of public transportation to get us to the embassy.

First we needed a way to get past the police and the hotel staff in order to get on the shuttle. The embassy had told us to do whatever we had to in order to get out of that hotel. I thought if we acted like we knew what we were doing and told them that we needed to run over to the airport to get everything set up for our flights home, they might not be as suspicious. "You never know until you try," was my first thought, so I told everyone my plan. We checked to see what times the shuttle ran so that we could all get downstairs and outside right as it was arriving. Just to be safe, we split up and left out of several different exits, so they wouldn't be as suspicious, and agreed to meet around at the front by the shuttle just as it pulled up.

Sure enough though, as I was walking out of the hotel, a policeman stopped me and asked where I was going. As nonchalantly as I could, I said, "Oh I'm just running over to the airport to change the tickets for our flights. It shouldn't take long and then I'll be back." Since I was walking straight toward the airport shuttle, it was apparently believable and he let me go. I met up with everyone else as we boarded the shuttle. My plan had worked! We were out of the hotel! We brought the Canadians out with us so that they could get to their embassy too.

We were all excited about finally escaping the hotel. It was as though we felt free, but at the same moment, we were a bit apprehensive about what might happen next. To help ease everyone's worries, I shared with them one of my favorite expressions: No expectations, no disappointments, so let's just stay positive and hopefully everything will work out. Once we got to the airport, there were taxis everywhere. Apparently we had either been lied to about the strike, or it was the most pathetic taxi strike ever. There was certainly no shortage of them at the airport. So we hailed a couple of cabs and had them take us to the American embassy.

- -

CHAPTER:

TWENTY-EIGHT

NAME:

DEBBIE

DATE:

1/14/12, MORNING EST

- -

My friend and I had seats booked on a flight later in the day, but the airlines had put us on the standby list and told us they should be able to get us on the first flight out that morning, so I knew we needed to be at the airport as early as possible. My friend got a few hours of sleep before we were up and ready to go a little before 4:00 a.m. We were leaving out of Fort Lauderdale instead of Miami, so we had a little bit of a drive. I figured if we got there around 4:30, we would have time to drop off the rental car and get checked in early so that we could be on the standby list.

On the way to the airport, my phone rang. It was my mom's cousin, whom I had been in contact with several times over the course of the evening. When I answered, the first thing she said to me was, "Debbie, they're okay. They're all okay. Your mom called me." I was relieved to hear it, but oddly enough, I couldn't completely believe it yet. I needed to see them myself or at least hear all of their voices. I knew Mom had called her cousin because she has a landline and is more likely to answer in the middle of the night. (And we are all so used to calling each other from our cell phones—with the numbers programmed in—that I'm not sure how many of us know each other's cell phone numbers by heart.) So while I understood why Mom didn't call me, I still wanted and needed to hear from them myself before I could truly relax.

I was very grateful, though, that I had received word of their safety before getting on a transcontinental flight and losing phone contact for five hours. Yet, I was still worried about them. Were they all physically okay? Were they mentally and emotionally okay? What all had they endured? As a social worker, I was even more concerned with their mental and emotional well-being because I've seen firsthand what traumatic events can do to people, even if they survive unscathed physically. While I was ecstatic to hear that they were okay, it felt like there was still so much that I didn't know.

Sure enough, just like the airlines had promised, we made it onto one of the earliest flights back to LA, so at least we didn't have to sit around the airport all day. Our plane had live in-flight news so I got to watch coverage of the wreck the entire way home. The sweet little older lady sitting next to me was watching it as well and at one point she turned to me and said, "Isn't that cruise ship thing horrible? I can't even imagine what those people are going through. It's just terrible." After talking about the wreck coverage with her for several minutes, I finally told her that my family had been on the ship. She was shocked and gave me a huge hug and told me it was going to be okay. It was nice to be sitting next to someone so sympathetic on that long flight. It made the trip a little more bearable.

I turned on my phone as soon as we landed and had fifteen voicemails and countless texts and emails waiting for me as we taxied into the gate. The sheer number of voicemails shocked me.

I didn't know if something had happened or what was going on. I scrolled through the list of phone numbers, thinking, "What the hell are all these New York numbers and why are they calling me?" I went straight to the strangest-looking number on the list and clicked it to listen to the message, thinking surely it would be the one from Italy. Sure enough, it was my mom.

WHY WERE CNN AND FOX NEWS CALLING ME? I COULDN'T FIGURE OUT WHY THEY WANTED TO TALK TO ME. I KNEW THE SHIPWRECK WAS MAJOR NEWS, BUT IT HADN'T DAWNED ON ME THAT SINCE MY FAMILY HAD BEEN ON THAT SHIP, THEY WERE MAJOR NEWS AS WELL.

I could tell she was crying and emotional. Her message said that they were all okay. I thought I could hear Cindy on the phone as well. As much as I'd wanted to hear from my mom, even hearing her voice say that they were all okay didn't alleviate my fears like I'd thought it would. My mom (as a mother) tries not to freak any of us out and I was worried that maybe someone *was* hurt and she just didn't want to tell me on the phone or leave it in a message. I just desperately wanted to hear everyone's voices and see all of them. I knew I couldn't even begin to relax until I had heard all four of their voices. I had never heard my mom sound so shaken before, and that probably played into my fears. I was still so nervous that someone wasn't okay that tears of relief weren't possible yet. I was also probably exhausted from not getting any sleep.

Moving on to the other fourteen calls on my voicemail log, I discovered that most of them were from the media. I was confused. Why were CNN and Fox News calling me? I couldn't figure out why they wanted to talk to me. I knew the shipwreck was major news, but it hadn't dawned on me that since my family had been on that ship, they were major news as well. Since I couldn't understand why they wanted to talk to me, and I didn't really care at that point, I just figured I would deal with those messages later. I also wasn't aware yet that my family had talked to an AP reporter in Italy, making our family even bigger news because of just how crazy and unbelievable their escape from the ship had been.

Besides all the news stations, I also had a message from my Aunt Bessie. Apparently someone had told her about the wreck. I remember being a little annoyed by that at first because I had wanted to tell her in person as soon as I got back to California. Once I discovered that the press had been trying to contact the family since 5:00 a.m., though, I was glad someone had told her. It would have been horrible for her to find out from the media.

When we finally got to the gate, I was in a rush to get off the plane and see Jonathan and try to help get my family back home. Usually I'm not in that big of a hurry to get off of a plane, so I'll sit and wait for it to clear out instead of trying to get my bags first and fight the crowds. But this time I jumped up quickly and grabbed my carry-on. I guess it was in some guy's way because he shoved it into me and I almost went flying backwards down the aisle. From out of nowhere, the cute little elderly lady that I had been sitting next to was suddenly up in his face *screaming* at him!

"Did you know that her family was on that cruise ship that

sank? Did you know that they almost died? You need to move out of her way!" She really let him have it! What a fireball!

And just like that, the seas parted and everyone got out of my way and I was able to get down the aisle and off the plane without a single incident. Thank God for that woman. People like that renew my faith in human beings. I will never forget watching her take on that big guy on my behalf. What an amazing little lady.

Other than the couple from New York that Valerie and I had met on the bus ride to Rome, we hadn't seen another American since the whole ordeal began. Granted, there were less than two hundred of us on the entire cruise ship, but I had still thought they would have grouped us by nationality, or at least language, at the various hotels to make it easier to get us in touch with our embassies and communicate with us. Unfortunately, my suspicion was that Costa had purposely split us up. When we got to the embassy, my suspicion grew even stronger.

We met a lot of the other Americans from the ship at the embassy when we arrived, and sure enough, they had been scattered to various hotels all over Rome. It wasn't just that we had been separated from other Americans—Americans had been spread out so that very few of us were together. Maybe it was just a big coincidence, but it certainly didn't seem like it to me. We weren't surprised to find out that more Americans had encountered obstacles in getting to the embassy too.

I had been a little discouraged when the American embassy

would not send someone to us at the hotel, especially considering we were having such issues trying to get to them, but when we got there everyone was incredibly nice and helpful. I'm still not sure why a representative couldn't have come to our hotel, though. Other embassies had sent people to help the survivors from their respective countries. Maybe it was for safety purposes or maybe the American embassy simply didn't have the manpower. Whatever the reason, it was a little disappointing.

Our family and friends had been on the phone with the State Department for several hours now, so the agents at the embassy were well aware of who we were and what our needs might be. They had contacted doctors and gotten our prescriptions called in ahead of time. While we waited on our temporary passports to be processed, I told them about our treatment by Costa and how, in addition to refusing to let us leave the hotel, they had also fed us a meager lunch, given us no clothes, and generally treated us horribly. We weren't the only passengers with stories of poor treatment, either.

When I mentioned that they hadn't even tried to get Cindy a jacket, one of the agents handed Cindy her own beautiful fur coat. At first Cindy didn't want to accept it because it was just too nice of a coat, but the agent insisted that she wear it and keep it. We tried to give it back when we were getting ready to leave, but she refused to take it back. She and Cindy went back and forth for several minutes, with Cindy refusing to keep it and the agent refusing to take it back. But when the agent told Cindy that she wanted her to leave Italy with at least one good memory of generosity, Cindy couldn't say no to that. It was such a sweet gesture and incredibly generous of her.

Dean had left his sweatshirt on the bus to Rome, but there was a really nice Marine from Las Vegas who gave Dean his sweatshirt. Overall, the people we met there were thoughtful and considerate. I think we were just very grateful to finally be around other Americans. It made the embassy feel a little more like the homes we were so desperate to get back to. We all had stories to share of getting off the ship and being treated poorly by the Costa cruise line, so being among fellow Americans was such a relief. And it was refreshing to be treated decently again. Many of the others were distraught at what they had been through; and all of us were eager to get our passports and get out of Italy.

It took several hours for them to get everything in order and get our temporary passports ready for us. Once they were ready, we were sent to a nearby pharmacy where our prescriptions were waiting for us. They had Dean's blood pressure medicine as well as a refill of the medication that Cindy's doctor had given her to help calm her nerves when flying.

We hadn't eaten much other than the meager lunch we had been given at the hotel. There was a quaint little Italian restaurant close to the pharmacy, and we figured we had better eat a decent dinner since we wanted to get a flight out as early as possible the next morning. Once again, we were grateful that Dean had taken a nap with his wallet still in his pocket since it meant we had cash for food and taxis! Valerie and Cindy shared a dish and said it was amazingly good. Oddly enough, I don't remember exactly what I had, but I remember it being delicious. Maybe it was because we hadn't had a real meal since the buffet lunch on the ship the day before, but our meal that night was one of the highlights of our short time in Italy.

We took a taxi back to our hotel after dinner. Since we hadn't exactly gotten to do any sightseeing on our drastically shortened trip to Italy, we asked the cab driver to take us by the Colosseum so that the girls could at least see it. They really enjoyed getting to drive by it, even at night, and it was so beautiful all lit up. For Cindy, the image of the Colosseum at night is one of the few positive memories she has of our disastrous trip. We were all a little sad to think of everything we had missed getting to see and do, but Dean said that we'd come back some day and make up for this trip. I highly doubt that we will do it on a ship though.

CHAPTER:

THIRTY

NAME:

DEBBIE

DATE:

1/14/12, LATE MORNING-EVENING PST

The plan was that Jonathan would pick me up at the airport and my friend's family would pick her up, that way Jonathan and I could go straight to my parents' house from LAX. I'd told him to grab all of his books for class and about a week's worth of clothes for both of us so that we could just set up camp at Mom and Dad's house while we dealt with this whole ordeal. I didn't want to worry about having to run back and forth to our place to change clothes or shower in the middle of trying to get my family back home. Jonathan and I only live about twelve miles from my parents, but with LA traffic, that can be an hour and a half at times. I just didn't want to mess with it.

We had just gotten in the car to head to their house from the airport when my mom called again. I asked to hear everyone's voices so that I could know for sure that they were all alive and well. I was relieved to hear Mom, Dad, Cindy, and Val all tell me that they were okay. Finally I could relax a little, but I knew I wouldn't be completely at ease until they were all home and I could hug each of them and see them with my own eyes.

WHEN WE PULLED UP AT MY PARENTS' HOUSE,
THE FULL EXTENT OF THE MEDIA INVOLVEMENT
HIT ME. THERE WERE NEWS VANS IN FRONT
OF THE HOUSE FROM ALL OF THE LOCAL NEWS
STATIONS.

Unfortunately we didn't get to talk long. I think they were at the embassy trying to get everything straightened out. I did get to tell them all how much I loved them and that I couldn't wait to see them again.

I'm not normally a skeptical person, but this whole thing had really shaken me up, and even hearing each individual's voice hadn't managed to make me completely believe that they were all okay. I knew they were all alive and able to talk and at the hotel, but I didn't know if anyone was injured and they didn't want to tell me or if they were more upset by the wreck than they were letting on. I needed to see them. I needed them home.

When we pulled up at my parents' house, the full extent of the media involvement hit me. There were news vans in front of the house from all of the local news stations. I had never had any dealings with the press before and I didn't know what to expect, but seeing all those vans and cameras, combined with all the phone calls from reporters that I had already received, sent me straight into protection mode. I had no idea if my parents or sisters had talked to the media yet or not, and I didn't know if they even wanted to. It became my mission to protect them from the media circus as long as I could. I didn't know what their mental state was and I wasn't about to risk upsetting them more than they probably already were by having people shove microphones and cameras in their faces as soon as they got home.

I didn't even want to worry my family by telling them how intense the media presence was at the house. For now, Jonathan and I would deal with it because we didn't want to add more stress to an already stressful situation. I have to admit, though, I never expected the press to be so accommodating. Not long after I got off the phone with the family, my phone rang again (basically it didn't stop ringing for the next two weeks). The reporter on the line told me he had just interviewed one of my dad's family members who has had nothing to do with my father or our family for many years. I must have been inspired by the little elderly lady on the plane, Because I told him in no uncertain terms that if he was going to speak to *anybody*, it was going to be me and only me—Debbie Ananias—who could speak on behalf of the family. I told him that once I ascertained what my family was comfortable doing I would cooperate with the press, but if he, or anyone else, tried to talk to any other family members but me, they would not be granted any interviews at all. After that, not a single reporter or news station contacted anyone but me. Apparently, news really does travel fast when the press is involved.

Overall, the reporters that had gathered at the house were a very polite bunch. I didn't want to make any comments at the time, mainly because I had no idea how my family felt about speaking to the media, but I told Jonathan if he wanted to give them a short statement, he could. He gave them enough to keep them happy for a while, and really, they didn't bother us again. They didn't leave though, although no one was pushy or in our face or acted at all like I had always assumed they would. Even the messages I was getting on my phone were very polite. My instructions to the one reporter about talking to anyone but me were being respected—I didn't have to tell that to any other reporter. It was really surprising. You always hear how annoying the press can be when they are after a story, but to me, they were very polite and respectful of our time and space.

My primary goal was to get my family home. I really didn't want to deal with the media, even though they were being as nice as possible, so I told Jonathan that he was in charge of handling the press. He fielded my phone calls and manned the front door when new reporters would show up and want to talk to us. He was amazing. I could focus on the family and not worry about my phone ringing off the hook. I hadn't been able to talk to my family long enough to know if they had been issued new passports yet or anything like that. I also had no way to get ahold of them so, for the most part, I was in the dark about everything and trying to coordinate as much as I could without being able to talk to them.

I spent most of my time on the phone with the cruise line and the U.S. embassy and anyone else I could think of to get information and help get my family home. No one was being especially helpful. I tried to be patient as long as I could, but at one point, I finally snapped when talking to a Costa representative. I had called the cruise line and asked what was being done to help my family. The representative was aware of the wreck and everything that had happened, but when I asked what steps the company was taking, I got the dumbest response anyone could possibly give. She asked me why my family hadn't *told* anyone that they disembarked the vessel. Really?

"Because the fucking boat was sinking!" I yelled. "Who the hell were they going to tell?" I continued to scream at her for a few minutes and I'm sure she thought I was completely insane, but I just couldn't handle any more incompetence from Costa. I am generally a pretty calm person in high-stress situations, probably due to my professional training, but when you add the stress of the situation and the complete stupidity of the comment, I just couldn't take it anymore. Dealing with someone that incompetent, at that point in time, was something I had neither the time nor the inclination to do.

At that point, I knew the cruise line was completely useless when it came to giving any type of assistance or even information. We hadn't received much more help from the embassy, but at least they had heard from us so many times over the course of the night and morning that, by the time the family got there, the agents knew who they were and what they needed. Unfortunately, they never did call us back after my family showed up like they had assured us they would. It didn't take me long to figure out that we were not going to get any help to get everyone home. We were on our own.

As a social worker, you quickly learn to become very resourceful and negotiate in order to advocate for others. With that in mind, a little bell went off in my head. The news media was *desperate* for anything we would give them. Maybe they would be willing to help me out in return for an interview. I had already seen how plugged in they were when I had told one reporter to leave the family alone and it had immediately been passed along to all the others. I had actually learned more from the news media than I had from either Costa or the embassy, including the name of the hotel where my family was staying. By this time, I knew my family had talked to an Associated Press reporter and, although I hadn't had time to read any of the articles to know what they had said, I knew they weren't completely opposed to talking to the press.

I had gotten a call from the *Today Show* and actually talked to one of the producers myself. She was very sweet, which I knew was partly because she wanted a story, but I appreciated how kind she was about it. During the conversation, she asked me, "What do you need?" I told her, "I need my family home." And she said she would help me get them home. Just like that. If I would give her their information, she would get them booked on a flight and get them home.

I knew this meant we owed her an exclusive, but I told her that I couldn't promise my family would be in any state for an interview when they got home. I warned her I needed to talk to them first and since I had no way to get ahold of them, I would have to wait until they called me back. I had tried calling the hotel (once a reporter told me where they were, since Costa wasn't competent enough to give me that information), but it would just ring and ring. The few times someone picked up, I was put on eternal hold while they tried to "connect me to my family." When I did finally talk to the family again, my mom said she didn't want to fly to New York—she and the family just wanted to get home, and they didn't have any plans at the moment, so she would have to get back to me. They were all so grateful for the *Today Show* being willing to help though, that they said they would go ahead and do the interview. They also (and more importantly) wanted people to know what had happened to them. That concerned me a little and I asked what exactly *had* happened, but they promised to fill me in once they got home. I worried that they really weren't okay to do an interview right after getting home.

While working on my master's degree in social work, I had taken a class at the University of Southern California about working with members of the military and their families. Post-Traumatic Stress Disorder (PTSD) and Acute Distress Disorder were covered in great detail as many military members and their families have experienced the effects of these disorders, so I know the signs and symptoms. I found myself analyzing everything my family said and did to figure out if they were okay—a natural reaction for someone who works in the field of mental health. I knew that reliving an ordeal by talking about it too soon after the event might not always be helpful. I didn't know if they would want to rehash their experience in the public arena immediately after getting home. I didn't think they were aware of the magnitude of the media presence at the house. My job skills and the intense situation at the house made me even more

I FELT LIKE BOTH THE PROTECTOR OF THE FAMILY AND THE ONE WHO HAD KIND OF BEEN LEFT OUT OF THE LOOP. IT WAS A WEIRD POSITION TO BE IN, AND I GUESS IT'S WHAT EVERYONE GOES THROUGH AS THEY WAIT FOR A FAMILY MEMBER TO RETURN FROM WAR OR ANY TRAGIC EVENT.

protective of my family.

Considering my dad's blood pressure issues, I was the most concerned for his physical health, but I also knew his navy training probably made him pretty capable of dealing with the emotional and mental strain. He served in the Vietnam War and was a teacher at an inner-city middle school in Los Angeles for almost thirty years. He's no stranger to stressful situations. But physically, I didn't know how he had fared with his blood pressure being such a concern. What if he had to overexert himself? Would his body hold up after such a stressful and physically demanding ordeal?

Jonathan figured I would be the most worried about Val, since she is usually the most sensitive and emotional person in the family, but I knew Val was a rock when push came to shove, and I had no doubt that she was fine. As a worrier, Val had probably played out every bad situation that could ever happen in her head and worked out exactly what to do in every case. So when she was actually put into one of those situations, her mental preparedness would have kicked in and she would have been totally ready to attack every challenge head-on. She was fine—I had no doubt.

I had no idea what they had physically endured, but I was worried that it might have been too much for my mom, since she is very strong mentally, but is very petite physically. She exercises regularly but is not the most athletic person. Turns out she had met every obstacle head-on as well, but at the time, I was worried the ordeal had been too hard on her. I knew Cindy and Val were pretty agile and could have handled whatever they were up against. Really, I was the most worried for my parents. They're in pretty decent shape for their ages, but I didn't know how their bodies would respond to the demands of getting off of a sinking ship, or even what all that had entailed.

Of course, I was incredibly concerned about everyone's mental well-being, but Cindy is the baby of the family, and it's only natural to worry more about the baby. Plus, she's already afraid of flying. I couldn't imagine how traumatized she must be to have lost the safe feeling she was used to having on ships. I figured they were probably all very traumatized about ships by now. I was, and I hadn't even been on that disastrous cruise.

I felt like both the protector of the family and the one who had kind of been left out of the loop. It was a weird position to be in, and I guess it's what everyone goes through as they wait for a family member to return from war or any tragic event. You feel like you can't possibly know what they must have gone through, and at the same time, you're determined to keep anything or anyone from causing them any more stress than they are already under. But there is only so much you can do in that situation, other than worry and shield them from everyone and everything you can.

Throughout the entire ordeal that day at the house, what surprised me the most was that the media was the only reliable source of information for me. I couldn't count on the government or the cruise line to keep me up to speed, but I could always count on the reporters that called (or were outside) to have the latest information about my family and the accident. I never expected to be so grateful for the press. Jonathan spoke to most of them when they called, getting their information and writing it down, but all of them were very polite and understanding and as helpful as possible. Basically the opposite of everyone else I dealt with in my struggle to help get my family home.

CHAPTER:

THIRTY-ONE

NAME:

CINDY

DATE:

1/14/12, NIGHT–
1/15/12 EVENING CET-EST

We got back to the hotel after getting our passports and eating dinner. I had loved even the short opportunity to see the Colosseum. At least I could leave Italy and take the image of that with me, instead of just thoughts of everything bad that had happened. Considering what all we had originally planned to see and do on that trip, I guess seeing the Colosseum at night for only a few minutes probably should have been a letdown, but honestly, it was the one shining moment for me that stands out when I think back on those horrible two days.

Luckily we hadn't been missed at the hotel so there was no one to yell at us for sneaking out. I remember feeling pretty disgusting by that point, since we were still in the same clothes we'd been in for dinner on the ship and hadn't gotten to shower or even brush our teeth. I guess I thought maybe Costa or the hotel or the embassy would have given us some clean clothes to wear, but apparently not.

As soon as we got back to our room, we started taking turns showering. It felt really great to be clean, right out of the shower.

CONSIDERING WHAT ALL WE HAD ORIGINALLY
PLANNED TO SEE AND DO ON THAT TRIP, I
GUESS SEEING THE COLOSSEUM AT NIGHT FOR
ONLY A FEW MINUTES PROBABLY SHOULD HAVE
BEEN A LETDOWN, BUT HONESTLY, IT WAS THE
ONE SHINING MOMENT FOR ME THAT STANDS
OUT WHEN I THINK BACK ON THOSE HORRIBLE
TWO DAYS.

But then it felt really gross to put the same dirty clothes back on. These weren't just your standard dirty clothes either. They were dirty clothes that we had worn on the side of the ship, and out in the rain on Giglio, and on the floor of a toy store, and on two separate buses.

We called Debbie again after we got back from the embassy and I got to talk to her for a minute. It was so good to hear my sister's voice, even though we didn't have much time to talk. None of us wanted to frighten her or the rest of the family, so we didn't tell her much about the details of everything we had been through. Mom told her we would fill her and the rest of the family in as soon as we got home. Debbie warned us that there was a lot of press at the house. Mom told her to call the local police department if it got too crazy so that they could at least help control the mass of reporters that were all up and down our street.

Debbie also told my mom that she had talked to someone at the *Today Show* and that they had offered to fly us, first class, to

New York and get us home from there (although we would need to give them an interview, it seemed). We really didn't want to go to New York—we wanted to go straight home—so Mom told her we'd have to get back to her about the tickets. We thought we would probably just use our own tickets to get home, if we could change them from the original date. Turns out we should have taken the *Today Show* up on their offer—it might have saved us the extra drama we had to deal with to get home. We did agree to go ahead and do an interview with them though, since they had been kind enough to offer, and we really wanted to tell our story so that people would know the truth about what had happened to us and the others on the *Costa Concordia*.

Right after we returned to the hotel, the manager phoned our room to tell us that the press had been calling nonstop, which was still really confusing for us, since we didn't consider ourselves newsworthy. When Mom talked to one of the news stations, she told them that we were exhausted and just wanted to get home and weren't doing any interviews until then. But they were nice enough to ask if we needed anything, and Dad asked if they could get us the phone number for Delta Air Lines so that we could call and get our flights changed, which they did. For some reason, we consistently got more help from the press than we did from the company whose ship sank out from under us.

Costa had told us that they would arrange for our flights home, but they had made no moves to get our information or even start the process, so we figured we'd better do it on our own. (Mom thought they wanted to keep us all there for a while longer to contain the situation and basically do damage control.) After my shower I called Delta to see if they had anything back to the United States the next day and was told they could get us out the next morning at 9:00 a.m. They waived the change fee so it didn't cost us anything. At least we were faring better with the airlines than we had with anyone else. We even managed to get seats together. I should have known it was just too perfect.

Once we had our flights all lined up and everyone had showered, we called Debbie back to give her the information and to talk to her for a few minutes again. She said she and some of the other family would meet us at the airport the next night. We all said we loved each other and couldn't wait to be back together again.

SHE TOLD US LATER THAT SHE JUST COULDN'T BELIEVE THAT AFTER WE HAD FOUND OUR OWN WAY OFF OF THEIR SINKING SHIP, FOUND OUR OWN PLACE TO SPEND THE NIGHT IN THE RAIN, FOUND OUR OWN (SLIGHTLY SNEAKY) WAY TO OUR EMBASSY, AND FOUND AND PAID FOR OUR OWN DINNER THE NIGHT BEFORE, THAT THE CRUISE LINE WAS TOO CHEAP TO PAY FOR US TO HAVE A HOT BREAKFAST.

After that, we had nothing to do but get through the night until we could leave for the airport the next day and get out of Rome. I think I slept for a couple of hours that night, but I'm not sure anyone else did—everyone was still on edge. Mom had tried to get us clothes and toothbrushes and toothpaste earlier but Costa said they were all out of everything—not the first time we'd heard that.

Since taking care of our personal hygiene wasn't an option and sleep was hard to come by, we basically just talked all night until it was time to get something to eat and head over to the airport.

Once it was officially morning, we gathered up our stuff, which consisted of picking up our temporary passports and Dad's wallet, and headed down to the lobby for breakfast. We weren't hungry but we knew we needed to get some nourishment before heading out on a long flight home. We got downstairs and saw this amazing, hot breakfast all spread out on buffet tables, with waffles and eggs and bacon and anything you could possibly want. When we went over to get our plates and go through the line, though, this guy walked up to Mom and asked if we were from the *Costa Concordia*. She said yes we were, and he told her they had a "special" room for us. We thought it was pretty nice of them to give us our own buffet and private room to eat in so we didn't have to deal with the crowds and the questions and everything else. Maybe they were finally going to start treating everyone better. So we headed over to our "special" dining room where we saw our "special" buffet—orange juice, coffee, and croissants. Mom refused to accept the breakfast they were giving us while the other hotel guests got the regular hot breakfast. She said she wasn't going to accept this kind of treatment and set off in search of a way to fix it. She found the hotel manager on duty and asked why the passengers were stuck in a room eating the "special" breakfast buffet. He told her he was really sorry but that Costa hadn't wanted to pay for any of the passengers to have the buffet. At that point, my mom was so mad that she burst into tears. She told us later that she just couldn't believe that after we had found our own way off of their sinking ship, found our own place to spend the night in the rain, found our own (slightly sneaky) way to our embassy, and found and paid for our own dinner the night before, that the cruise line was too cheap to pay for us to have a hot breakfast.

I guess the manager had been involved in a disaster once himself (a bombing, I think) and knew how hard it was to be in our shoes. So when Mom started crying, he started apologizing over and over and told her he would cover our breakfast even if Costa wouldn't. He said we could have anything we wanted, on the Hilton. Mom tried to refuse it because the point was Costa should have been paying for the breakfast and offering it to all of the passengers. The manager was so sweet though and begged her to let him feed us a decent meal. She didn't think it was fair to the other survivors there, but he insisted on at least giving us the hot breakfast. We could all tell how hurt and upset Mom was though at the blatant snub by Costa. It was the epitome of rudeness in a long line of rude treatment.

After we ate our breakfast, we needed to engineer our way out of the hotel again. Mom had us all go get on the airport shuttle before she turned in the keys, just in case something happened and we couldn't get out. Once we were all outside on the bus, she went up to the counter, handed over our room keys, and told them that the Ananias family was checking out and to make a note of that in case anyone asked. Then she bolted out the door and jumped on the shuttle with us. We all breathed a huge sigh of relief to finally be leaving the hotel where we had been treated like criminals since our arrival the day before.

We got to the airport and got in line to check in for our flight, which is pretty simple when you don't have bags to check or carry on. When we gave them our temporary passports and told them the flight we were on, our bad luck came back in full force. The agent said she didn't have a record of us on that flight. I knew that couldn't be right because I had *just* changed the tickets the night before. But she insisted that our names weren't on that flight. The agent asked for our confirmation number, so I gave it to her. Sure enough, when she looked it up, it showed us on that flight, at that time of day—but for the following month! No wonder it had been so easy to get seats together; apparently we were leaving in February and not January.

I guess the ticket agent on the phone didn't check the month when she put the change request in and it defaulted to the next month, since that was our original departure month. So now we were at the Rome airport, checked out of the hotel, but we didn't have a flight for that day—or that month. I just couldn't believe it. It was like some cruel joke.

I explained our situation to the agent and she was really sympathetic once she heard we had been on the *Costa Concordia*. She had her supervisor come over and told him the whole story, and we were put on the standby list for that day. They said they would do whatever they could to get us back to the States within twenty-four hours. At least it wasn't just the media and the hotel manager who were trying to be helpful.

By some miracle, they got us on that first flight out—the one we thought we were already on. They had actually asked other passengers to switch their flights so that they could get us on that plane. We even got little bags with toothbrushes and toothpaste, since Costa hadn't bothered to provide us with those. The Delta employees in Italy were some of the nicest people we met there. They escorted us through the airport and said they were so sorry for everything we had been through. You could tell they really felt horrible and were just nice, caring employees who did anything and everything to help out their customers.

Valerie and I were lucky enough to get seats together but Mom and Dad had to sit somewhere else. Before we got on the plane, everyone had grabbed some over-the-counter sleep aides since no one had really slept much in the past thirty-six hours (not since our naps on Friday—and Mom hadn't even taken a nap). I took some medication for my flying anxiety, although my desire to get home and the events of the past two days had greatly reduced my fear of being on that plane. Luckily, our meds worked and we were all lights-out for the entire flight back to Atlanta, except for Dad. He said he just couldn't get his mind to turn off enough to sleep.

Val isn't used to taking anything to help her sleep, so she was totally knocked out by it. According to her, she woke up at some point in the flight and noticed we were both curled up peacefully in our seats, but she was still too groggy to notice much else. Poor Val—she rarely even takes something when she's sick, so I'm sure it was weird for her to feel that out of it, but at least she finally got some sleep—and at least we didn't seem bothered by the usually uncomfortable airline seats.

That was the first flight I can ever remember taking where I wasn't terrified or anxious to be flying. I just wanted to get home and put this nightmare behind me. Being on the shipwreck had been so draining, physically and emotionally, that I just didn't care about being on a plane at that point. Since the accident, my flying anxiety has come back some, but not to the extent it was before the *Costa Concordia*. I'm not really sure why. Maybe it's because I know worrying or not worrying isn't going to change anything. If something is going to happen, it's going to happen, regardless of how anxious I am or not. I don't know if I'll ever feel completely safe on a plane (certainly not on a ship), but I do feel better now than I did before.

We had assumed that our bad luck would change as soon as we were back on American soil, but that didn't exactly happen. We had a huge layover between coming in from Rome and leaving for

LA, so once we got to the Atlanta airport, we asked if there was a way to get us on an earlier flight out. As nice and accommodating as the Delta employees had been in Rome, they were equally *not* nice and accommodating in Atlanta. They didn't care about what we had been through or that we hadn't changed clothes in two days—they weren't going to put themselves out to get us home any sooner. And they weren't apologetic about it either. In fact, they were downright rude. How ironic that in our own country we were treated worse by the employees of an American company than we were in Italy. I think it actually made us feel worse dealing with this in our own country.

It wouldn't have been a big deal if they had at least been polite about it or said they would see what they could do, but to be rude was just ridiculous. We weren't trying to change our flight for some superficial reason or just to be difficult. We had been on a ship that sank and we just wanted to get back to our home. It seemed like a pretty reasonable request to us that they at least *try* to fit us on something earlier. Apparently it wasn't. I didn't fare much better when I called to complain about the rude gate agent—all I got was a rude customer service agent.

We knew we had an interview with the *Today Show* really early in the morning in LA, so we wanted to get home as soon as possible to try to spend some time with Debbie and the rest of the family before the interview, but it just wasn't going to happen. We had to settle for the flight later in the day, which would put us back in California that night around 10:00 p.m. We talked to Debbie again while we waited for our flight and she told us that there was a special plan to get us out of LAX so that we didn't get bombarded with the press. Finally it was time for our flight to leave and we settled back in for the last few hours until this whole mess was over and we could finally say we were home.

CHAPTER:

THIRTY-TWO

NAME:

DEBBIE

DATE:

1/15/12

By Sunday morning, the news-station reporters and vans were piling up in front of the house and starting to make waves about being at the airport when the family arrived that night. I had already talked to Mom about it, and the family was adamant that they didn't want to deal with the press at the airport. I told the reporters about the family's request and they said that was no problem, they wouldn't go to the airport, but I wanted to make sure my family's wishes were honored. The reporters had stayed respectful of all of my requests up until that point, but I didn't want to risk this being the one time they didn't honor their promise.

On Sunday, Jonathan and I spent the day going to the store to get some of the basics that I thought the family might need when they got home. Because they had been planning such a long trip, they had taken everything with them (instead of just buying travel sizes), so they had no toothpaste, toothbrushes, soap, or shampoo—basically they needed a total restock of all toiletries, since theirs were sitting underwater in the Mediterranean Sea. I wanted to do whatever I could to make things as calm and easy as possible for their homecoming. There was also very little food in the house, again due to the planned length of the trip. Needless to say, the list was long.

IT WAS SO WEIRD TO THINK OF IT, BUT JUST A WEEK AND A DAY BEFORE, WE HAD BEEN AT MY WEDDING, CELEBRATING MY MARRIAGE TO JONATHAN. LESS THAN A WEEK LATER I HAD BEEN DEVASTATED, THINKING I HAD LOST MY ENTIRE FAMILY IN A SHIPWRECK. AND NOW HERE WE ALL WERE AGAIN, OVERJOYED TO BE WELCOMING THEM BACK HOME.

When it was finally time to pick them up, we worked out a plan to get the family to the car without going through the main LAX exit just in case some of the media decided to show up. We had specifically not told them any flight details, but they still found out what flight my family was on and what time it was coming in, including the information that it was slightly delayed. I have no idea how they find that information out, but they're amazingly talented at it. It was a little unnerving that they could know so much, although at least it had benefitted me for the most part, since I had gotten the majority of my information from them over the past twenty-four hours.

There were a few of us there ready to welcome them when

they got off the plane, including my aunt and our close cousins. My grandmother wasn't able to understand what was going on, so we didn't want to confuse her by taking her. The whole family had been on such a crazy roller coaster of emotions over the past week. It was so weird to think of it, but just a week and a day before, we had been at my wedding, celebrating my marriage to Jonathan. Less than a week later I had been devastated, thinking I had lost my entire family in a shipwreck. And now here we all were again, overjoyed to be welcoming them back home. It is incredibly exhausting to experience such a wide range of strong emotions in such a short period of time.

I needed so badly to see them all again. It's very hard to explain but when you think you've lost loved ones and then find out you haven't, the need to be with them in person is overwhelming. I was anxious to see them, and of course, it felt like it took forever for them to get off that plane. When I finally did see them, I was like a little kid who could barely control my excitement. In fact, I got yelled at by security when I tried to get to them before they could exit the secured area to get to me! As soon as we all saw each other, the tears just started flowing. I was relieved to finally have them in front of me, and I know they were relieved to finally be home.

Cindy had on this crazy fur coat and I couldn't figure out where it had come from, and my dad had some maroon sweatshirt on from some random college—they definitely looked eclectic, to say the least. It would have been comical if I hadn't been so emotional over seeing them again.

Of course, I was still worried about what all they had been through, since they had told me so little. I didn't know what the long-term ramifications of this ordeal would be on them. At the time, they were just happy to be home and incredibly exhausted.

Val and Cindy were literally jumping up and down they were so thrilled to be home. I could tell Mom and Dad were relieved to have the past few days behind them. I also knew, from my training, that things really weren't over and that, to a large extent, the emotional and mental side of things was really just beginning.

Luckily they didn't have any baggage so they didn't need to go through the mess that is LAX's baggage claim. More than anything, I just wanted to get them home so that they could relax and fill us in on what they had been through. I was nervous to hear it, but I knew they needed to talk through it all with the family before they had to rehash it on live television in a few short hours for the *Today Show.*

I had wanted to get home so badly, basically ever since we first suspected something was wrong on the ship. Normally, I love traveling and being away from home. Coming home is usually the saddest part of a vacation for me. Not this time, though. Getting home was all I could think about. And I fully expected to break down and cry as soon as I saw Debbie and the rest of the family, considering how emotional of a person I normally am. Maybe it was the sleep aid still wearing off or maybe I was just totally drained after the previous couple of days, but I actually didn't cry at all. In fact, I was so overjoyed that I was literally jumping up

I HAD LITERALLY THOUGHT I WOULD NEVER
SEE THESE PEOPLE AGAIN (AT LEAST NOT ON
THIS EARTH), AND YET HERE THEY ALL WERE
IN FRONT OF ME.

and down in excitement! I was elated to see all the people I love so much, Debbie, my godparents, and my cousins. Cindy was as excited as I was and she was hugging everyone and jumping up and down with me. It was almost so amazing that it didn't feel real. It felt like a cross between a dream and an out-of-body experience—and I kept thinking it was too good to be true.

IT'S A DIFFICULT SITUATION TO BE IN— PEOPLE WANTED AND NEEDED TO KNOW WHAT HAD HAPPENED, BUT *WE* WANTED AND NEEDED TO JUST ENJOY BEING ALIVE AND HOME WITH OUR FAMILY.

I wanted to hug and kiss everyone and I wanted them to know how important they were to me and how much I loved them. It's funny how quickly you realize what's really meaningful in life when you're faced with losing it all. I had literally thought I would never see these people again (at least not on this earth), and yet here they all were in front of me—wonderfully in front of me. They were crying and hugging us back and everyone was trying to talk at once, but in a happy, excited-to-be-reunited way. They also kept telling us that we were all over the news and all over the Internet, but I was having a hard time grasping that part. I wasn't looking forward to facing the media. I just wanted to enjoy this special time with my family, not deal with the news crews that were stationed all over our neighborhood.

We didn't have any baggage to claim, so at least it was really simple to leave the airport. Debbie told us we had to go out a different way to hopefully avoid the reporters that were waiting for us at LAX. She'd been able to keep some from showing up, but inevitably, others were there in their place. Debbie had warned the press, though, that if they showed up at the airport, they'd never get an interview, since that was the time we all needed to just enjoy seeing each other again. We had to split up into a few separate cars to get back home, but at least the house wasn't that far from the airport, and we would all meet back there within a short time.

I knew the *Today Show* would be ready to interview us by 3:00 or 4:00 a.m. and we still had to get into hair and makeup before that. All I wanted, though, was to be with the people I loved. I wasn't at all excited to do a live interview, even though I knew people needed to hear what had happened to us. Maybe if I would have had a few days to unwind and process everything, it would have been easier. Then again, maybe a few days would have made me even more hesitant to mentally relive everything again. It's a difficult situation to be in—people wanted and needed to know what had happened, but *we* wanted and needed to just enjoy being alive and home with our family. I don't think there's an easy or "right" way to solve those conflicting needs, and I think that conflict is probably something that most survivors deal with after a disastrous tragedy.

I couldn't figure out how I was going to compose myself on national television when I felt so emotionally exhausted and totally wiped out. We had to be in business casual clothes with our hair done and makeup on; yet looking good for television just wasn't a priority right at that moment. I hadn't even changed clothes in three days! My looks were the last thing on my mind. Plus, half of my wardrobe and all of my makeup was at the bottom of the Mediterranean Sea, so even if I'd wanted to, I was limited in my ability to get all dolled up.

The idea that our story and the story of the *Costa Concordia* was such major news was still unbelievable to me. I had been surprised at the media presence in Rome, but I guess I thought maybe it was because the story was regional. I never imagined it was that huge back in the States, as well as worldwide. In fact, I had a dear family friend who was stationed in Afghanistan at the time and he told us he had seen what happened on the news coverage of the wreck on base—he had even seen our family on the news. Apparently, he almost dropped his food tray from the shock! He had seen some horrible stuff on his deployment and he was still floored over the news of the wreck. I guess I just didn't realize how newsworthy it was. Since then, several other cruising disasters have also been major news, so it makes sense to me now why the *Costa Concordia* was such a big deal. At the time though, I was just too close to the situation to really grasp it all.

When we got back to the house, we could see the media vans up and down the street, but thankfully they let us go in and get settled without accosting us. I thought it was very respectful of them and I really appreciated their consideration. Once we were all together again, we sat the family down and filled them in on everything that had happened to us since we had left on Thursday morning. It took three hours to go over our whole ordeal. It was clear from their faces how shocked they were at everything we had been through. Everyone tried to be very comforting and listen while we got it all out, but you could tell they were totally stunned by the series of events—from the initial impact, to our treatment by Costa and our difficulties in getting our flights straightened out.

As soon as we were done, it was time to start getting ready to tell it all again, this time with a camera filming it. The crew that showed up at the house was nice, pleasant, and supportive. Several people were visibly affected by our story. But it was still so draining to go through the whole process—I don't remember a lot of details from that night because I was just so exhausted. The crew came in and set everything up for the feed to New York. Meanwhile, I still couldn't believe this was happening and that I was about to be on a national morning news show.

The whole experience was crazy. Suddenly the house was transformed into a set with lighting and cameras and a full crew. It was so much to process. Of course, in the long run, it was a lot of effort for only a few minutes of interview time. And as draining as it all was, it turned out to be a good experience. Everyone was so kind and I've never regretted that we did that interview so soon after returning home. For some reason though, I thought that interview would be the end of things—but it wasn't. Debbie fielded all the reporters and news stations as they kept calling the house, and for whatever reason, a lot of them wanted to talk to me. Maybe it's because I had been the first one quoted by the AP reporter back in Italy, so my name was the first one of which they were aware. Regardless of the reasons, one thing was obvious—our story was big news—we were big news—and that wasn't changing after just one interview.

E veryone at home had been working frantically to get everything in order and ready for us when we got home—especially
Debbie. My cousin told me that Debbie had been a stalwart of
strength and energy and the rock that everyone else in the family
looked to for directions and stability during those difficult couple
of days. We didn't have to worry about having our medications
or Dean's sleep apnea machine—Debbie had taken care of it. We
didn't have to worry about food or toiletry items—Debbie had
taken care of it. And most importantly, we didn't have to worry
about being hounded by the reporters that were hanging around
everywhere because Debbie had taken care of that too. She was
truly amazing. As proud as I had been of my eldest and young-
est daughters while we suffered through that terrible ordeal on
the *Costa Concordia* and in Rome, I found myself equally proud
of my middle daughter upon returning home and hearing how
much she had done for us and how strong she had been.

We had agreed to do the *Today Show* interview that first night
(early morning) after we got home because we wanted people to

know what we had gone through and what had happened on the *Costa Concordia*. We were also appreciative of the fact that they were willing to get us out of Rome and back to the United States even though we didn't take them up on their offer. The phones never stopped ringing once we were at home, from our home phone to our business phones to Debbie's cell phone (and extended family members' phones as well). The *Today Show* interview had gone very well—they sent makeup and hair crews (although we struggled to find nice clothes to wear since so many of ours had been on the ship), but as far as everything else went, they made sure that things ran as smoothly as possible. I definitely felt a lot better on air for that interview than I had getting my temporary passport photo made only a short time before in Rome! It probably had as much to do with no longer feeling a sense of terror as it did with actually being showered and in fresh clothes and makeup.

SO MUCH HAD GONE WRONG ON THAT SHIP— SO MUCH THAT COULD EASILY HAVE BEEN HANDLED BETTER THAN IT WAS—AND IF WE DIDN'T TELL PEOPLE ABOUT IT, IT MIGHT HAPPEN AGAIN ON ANOTHER SHIP. WE FELT DESTINED TO BE THE VOICE FOR THOSE THAT HAD PERISHED THAT FATEFUL NIGHT.

We had gotten home late Sunday night on January 15. Upon arriving home, we spent three hours debriefing our family about what we had gone through. Up until that point, they knew nothing of the events of that night except what they had heard from the media. After filling them in, we slept for a couple of hours, and on Monday, January 16, at four o'clock in the morning, we geared up to do the *Today Show*. On Wednesday, we were scheduled to be on the Dr. Phil show. Later, we would also do interviews with both Dr. Drew and Anderson Cooper. In addition, we later participated in the documentaries about the cruise accident on the Discovery Channel as well as CNN's *Cruise to Disaster*. Our determination to share our story came mostly from those five hours that we had endured on the ship. There were several times we didn't think we would survive, and we told ourselves that if we did, there had to be a reason. So when we had the opportunity to tell the world what had happened to us on that disastrous night and speak for those that had died, we didn't feel that we could turn our backs. So much had gone wrong on that ship—so much that could easily have been handled better than it was—and if we didn't tell people about it, it might happen again on another ship. We felt destined to be the voice for those that had perished that fateful night.

Shortly after we got home, the reports began trickling in, claiming that the death toll was around ten. We knew good and well, from seeing body bags, that the death toll had to be higher than ten, and it felt to me that things were being smoothed over, either by Costa or some other entity, and it really irked me. I wanted people to know the truth. I was also very bothered emotionally, wondering what had happened to the Argentinian couple with the baby. We had not seen them again after we climbed down off of that railing, and I had no idea whether they had made it off the ship or not. I kept hoping that if we told the story of our encounter with them, someone could help us track them down to make sure they were okay, or maybe they would reach out to us. But neither happened. A year and a half later, I still don't know the fate of that young couple and their adorable little girl. I've actually checked the official manifest several times looking for a couple with a child about her age. Valerie remembered that her name was Valentina, and we found a little girl with that name, about three years old, on the list. But based on the names and ages of the passengers with her, it seemed she was traveling with her father and little brother, and we certainly never saw a little boy with the couple we met. The Valentina and her family on the list also weren't from Argentina. That whole situation is still one of the most bothersome mysteries to me about our entire experience—who were they, why did they hand me their daughter, and what happened to them? I may never know the answer and that torments me.

I HAVE LEARNED THROUGH ALL OF THIS THAT DOING SOMETHING (NO MATTER HOW BIG OR SMALL THE GESTURE) FOR A PERSON WHO HAS EXPERIENCED A TRAGEDY OF ANY KIND CAN BE THE BEST MEDICINE THAT PERSON CAN RECEIVE.

Those initial interviews following our homecoming were far easier than I thought they would be. Dean especially felt that talking about it was helpful. People were so understanding and empathetic to what we had been through and what our needs might be. The shows' crew members were always sensitive and kind, and if we ever seemed choked up or had a difficult time retelling something, everyone was very encouraging and supportive and gave us as much time as we needed. We all really appreciated the way that the media in general treated us. I was surprised again and again at how they never pushed or demanded anything of us and always put our concerns and needs at the forefront of every interview.

All of our wonderful family and friends reached out to us in so many ways after we returned home. The cards, letters, phone calls, emails, texts, food, flowers, plants, and visits were truly thoughtful. We were touched beyond words, but at the time, we were unable to visit with all the people that wanted to see us. We needed to save our energy to get the truth out and to set the record straight about the events of the *Costa Concordia*. It is amazing, though, what small gestures of love can mean to people who have suffered a tragic event. I have learned through all of this that doing something (no matter how big or small the gesture) for a person who has experienced a tragedy of any kind can be the best medicine that person can receive. Also, checking with him or her periodically through the months and years that follow can be very healing and comforting and goes a long way towards validating what they have gone through.

The Dr. Phil show was our second interview, and by that Wednesday, Valerie and Cindy just weren't feeling up to another major interview. The show suggested that Debbie come along instead, since she was such an important part of what had happened. The producers and Dr. Phil thought that people might like to hear her voice and what she went through at home, wondering if we were all right and then trying to help us get home and preparing for our arrival. I think it's easy to forget that, in a tragedy such as this, the victims aren't just the people directly involved. They're also the people at home, waiting and praying to hear news of their loved ones, hoping they will get to see them again. After the *Titanic* went down, thousands of people crowded into New York City hoping to hear the fate of a friend or family member. After the World Trade Center was attacked, people were desperate to get word from the people they knew who worked or lived near Ground Zero. Following the tragedies at Sandy Hook Elementary School and the Colorado theater, each entire community waited in a state of panic, hoping to hear that their children and family members were not among those massacred. Even after the recent Boston Marathon bombing, Americans with loved ones at or in the marathon worried as they watched the news coverage of the event but couldn't get through on the phone lines to those loved ones to make sure they were alive and well. Debbie's story is that of so many people who have had to endure the unknown, waiting to hear whether they will see someone again—or not.

It was also comforting for Dean and me to have Debbie there with us for the taping of that show. We had missed her so much when we were on the ship and had been so distraught over the idea that we might never see her again, that to have her with us when we got home became of paramount importance. She and Jonathan took off work to be with us as much as possible during those first days home. They stayed at the house with us and cooked for us and just looked after us in every way imaginable. And we relished every minute we spent with them.

Dr. Phil and Robin met with us before and after the show and I was able to tell him about how I was feeling (or really not feeling). It made those first few days and weeks so much better for me. It seemed like we were talking to family members because they displayed both care and compassion for what we had gone through. I told Dr. Phil that I could tell the story and recount every minute of what happened, but I couldn't emotionally feel what had happened. He explained that this was normal because my mind was protecting me from what had happened. He assured me that, in time, I would be able to emotionally connect to what I had been through. Hearing this from one of the most well-known psychologists in the world really helped to ease my mind about the healing process my family and I would be going through.

Our experiences with Dr. Drew and Anderson Cooper were positive as well. We were even able to discuss several issues with a CNN legal correspondent who was on air with us to give his legal insight into the circumstances surrounding the disaster. We also were interviewed by the U.S. Coast Guard and the National Transportation Safety Board (NTSB) from Washington, D.C. for four and a half hours. We were told that our interview would be utilized at the transportation committee hearings on the *Costa Concordia* accident, although we were never told the outcome of those hearings.

In the midst of our time spent with the press in those first few weeks, we also had to see doctors for our physical ailments as well as counselors to make sure we had started the healing process mentally. Physically and emotionally we were faced with a lot of challenges but we knew we would tackle them head on, just like we did when the disaster occurred. Thankfully, we were assisted by some excellent and dedicated professionals. Their insight, understanding, and compassion in helping us deal with the aftermath of this event have been essential to our healing process. Cruising had been an intricate part of our lives since our children were very young. We took several cruises a year, first with my parents, and later, on our own and with extended family members and friends. To have that key element of our family dynamic suddenly turned on its head was devastating. I had no idea if any of us would ever be in a place where we would feel comfortable getting on a cruise ship again. Would we even feel comfortable traveling internationally after what we had been through in Rome?

Complicating matters dramatically was our early contact with Costa Cruises. We had barely been home a day when we started receiving phone calls from the company. The calls were all the same in those early days (although some were in the middle of the night)—had we accepted their offer of thirty percent off of our next cruise? It's almost laughable now to think that we had barely gotten home from surviving a sinking cruise liner when the company started trying to appease us with offers for our next cruise. Our next cruise—it was something we couldn't even *fathom* at that point, and I'm not sure we even can now. I told them over and over to please stop calling because it was upsetting everyone in the family. They didn't stop—sometimes it was hourly and sometimes a few hours would pass in between calls—but they never stopped coming. Finally, I told them that if they called us one more time, we would call our attorney and take legal action against them for harassment.

Then the letters began arriving. The first letters were similar to the phone calls. Later, the stakes were raised—we were offered eleven thousand euros (the equivalent of about fourteen thousand, five hundred U.S. dollars), and we had to let them know by a certain date and sign the settlement and release agreement. When we didn't respond by that date, they sent us another letter with the same message except they extended the deadline date, trying to attract us again to sign on the dotted line. The settlement and release agreement meant that we were releasing all claims against Costa and Carnival Corporation

(Costa's parent company), their officers, directors, employees, crew, tour operators, and travel agencies.

Basically, if we signed the form, we were releasing them from liability for the loss of all our baggage and its contents (those are still on the ship to this day), personal effects, and—the big one—all damages of any kind. That included emotional and psychological distress, personal and property injuries, loss of income, and loss of enjoyment of the cruise that was caused by the result of the accident. The settlement and release agreement was governed by Italian law and consistent with the terms and conditions of the passage contract. The amount they were offering was also based on Italian and international law. It wasn't out of the kindness of their hearts; it was their legal obligation. I suspect that this same legal obligation is the reason that more cruise liners aren't evacuated even when they have fires, mechanical problems, or outbreaks of disease. If they were to evacuate the ship, they would owe every single passenger a monetary compensation similar to ours. The catch if you accept it is that you waive any other legal redress for what you went through.

While the cruise line was busy sending us these "offers" of money to settle, they were also running a subsequent media campaign telling everyone how generous they were being, offering the victims these settlement packages. They neglected to mention they were required by law to offer those packages. The settlement and release agreement was mailed out with each of those offers that Costa mailed out. Since accepting the offer meant signing away your right to sue for any further compensation, various consumer groups urged survivors not to accept this amount. Quite a few attorneys didn't seem to agree with Costa that it was an adequate compensation for the true damages suffered by those of us on the ship.

IN SEVERAL OF MY INITIAL INTERVIEWS, I
POINTED OUT THAT, YES THE CAPTAIN WAS
A LOOSE CANNON, BUT I WANTED TO KNOW
WHAT HAPPENED TO THE OTHER OFFICERS. WHY
DIDN'T SOMEONE STEP UP AND TAKE CHARGE?

Costa was also very busy running a smear campaign against the captain of the *Concordia*. He had deviated from the route, apparently "show-boating" (quite literally) to the citizens of Giglio. Rumor had it that he had done it a few weeks before as well. Not only had criminal charges been filed against him, but Costa was quick to point the finger at him, and only him, as the one solely responsible for the disaster. They didn't mention the lack of training (and pay) that they gave their crew or the way they treated survivors on the island and the mainland of Italy immediately following the wreck. They needed a scapegoat and the captain was perfectly suited to the role. In several of my initial interviews, I pointed out that, yes the captain was a loose cannon, but I wanted to know what happened to the other officers. Why didn't someone step up and take charge?

I'm in no way excusing what the captain did. Clearly, we were way too close to land for us to have run aground on those rocks like we did—he was blatantly negligent and reckless. And his behavior after the collision, refusing to evacuate the ship right away, ignoring the direct orders of the Italian Coast Guard to go back on the ship, and getting himself and his lady friend off before most of the passengers, is inexcusable. But he is not the only one at fault. The corporation hired him, trained him, and should have been aware that he was a loose cannon and that he had a tendency to party. Even the crew members we spoke with on Giglio seemed fully aware of how he was. Obviously, it wasn't a secret.

As if to add insult to injury, two weeks after the disaster my credit cards were stolen from my purse, which I had thrown down on the deck because I couldn't hold on to it. This was the ultimate slap in the face. I can't imagine that whoever it was that found my purse after I dropped it, in the midst of such a massive tragedy, decided to *steal* what was in it rather than return it, or even just leave it there on the ship. It's just unbelievable to me. But sure enough, one of my credit card companies contacted me after we were home to inform me that someone was buying Eurorail passes with my card. It was just one more annoyance we had to deal with on top of everything else we had been through. I had to make a report to the State Department, which was just another hassle, and then I had to change all my credit cards. It would have been so comforting to have had the contents of my purse back. I didn't even care if they took all the cash that was in it.

Yet the true icing on what had become a very bitter cake came a year later. We were still in contact with the Associated Press reporter who had done our very first interview and she asked if we were coming to Giglio for the one-year memorial services. We didn't know anything about it, but we had already contemplated going back to thank the people who had been so kind to us during our time in Italy, specifically the owners of the pharmacy and the toy store. I had already sent a letter to the owners of the toy store thanking them profusely for letting us stay in their store that night and being so welcoming. But we thought we might find some sort of closure in actually going back and visiting the site of the accident that had caused so much pain for our family.

We were curious about this anniversary memorial, so we asked Nicole to get us more information.

We learned the plan was to put a plaque on part of the rock that had been embedded in the ship and drop it back in the water to memorialize those that had died. Costa was organizing everything and they had planned a service at the church there on the island, as well as a concert that night. We were in the midst of trying to figure out if we were all going, or if just Dean and I would go when we received a letter from Costa. I immediately assumed it was a formal invitation to the memorial, but when I opened it up, I discovered quite the opposite. After some nice wording about remembering those that died, we came to the part of the letter that told us, point-blank, that we were not invited. Their reason had to do with the size of the island. Apparently they couldn't accommodate all of us.

IF THE WIND HAD NOT BLOWN THE SHIP IN THE DIRECTION OF THE SHORE, THE NUMBER OF DEATHS COULD POSSIBLY HAVE SURPASSED THE DEATH TOLL OF THE *TITANIC* DISASTER NEARLY ONE HUNDRED YEARS EARLIER.

I immediately called Nicole and filled her in. She was *shocked*. She wanted a copy of the letter. As it turned out, not everyone had received a letter—Costa had handpicked the people to specifically preclude from coming. Nicole wanted us to come anyway, knowing how important closure was to us, but I had no desire to stir the pot any further or drag my family through any more drama. Later, Costa changed their story and said that they would welcome anyone that wanted to come, although they didn't tell *us* that specifically.

Instead of spending the anniversary of the disaster in Italy, we decided to spend it in church, remembering those that had died and praying for their families. Then, in an attempt to turn that day around for our family and make it a joyous one, we headed to Disneyland. A dear family friend of the girls who works there treated us all to a day in the happiest place on earth. He even spent the day with us to ensure we had a great time. We needed happy memories to replace the traumatic ones we currently had of that day in our lives. At the exact moment of the impact with the rocks, our family stopped and said another prayer for those that had died and those that had survived a year before. Personally, I also said a special prayer for my brother Jim who had passed eleven years ago to that day.

I wish so desperately that our family could move on from what happened, but it is incredibly difficult to do when the criminal and civil trials are still ongoing, the salvage expedition is still in the works, and the news is still filled with cruise disaster after cruise disaster—all serving as reminders of what happened to us on that chilly January night. There's so much that we would like to see changed in the cruising industry so that no one else has to endure what we did. Things are not progressing as they should after a disaster that took the lives of over thirty people. If the wind had not blown the ship in the direction of the shore, the number of deaths could possibly have surpassed the death toll of the *Titanic* disaster nearly one hundred years earlier.

I can only hope that one day enough changes will have been

made in the cruise line industry, putting passenger safety above anything else, that my family can feel safe enough to again enjoy what used to be our favorite pastime, before we learned how quickly it could become our worst nightmare. I recognize mistakes happen in life, but what troubles me the most is that the cruise industry is not stepping up and doing what is right for the people who take future cruises. Oprah Winfrey said in her Harvard 2013 commencement speech, "Learn from every mistake because every experience, encounter, and particularly your mistakes are there to teach you and force you into being more of who you are." This disaster should be a lesson to be dealt with seriously and earnestly so that future travelers will have the safety they deserve. It seems to me that all the beauty and extravagant activities on board these luxury cruise lines take precedence over general passenger and cruising safety. Something needs to change and it needs to change now. Our experience on the *Costa Concordia* changed all of us and took something meaningful away from us, but it will not stop us from advocating for change, living our lives to the fullest, and continuing to appreciate all life has to offer.

THIRTY–FIVE

DEAN

REACTIONS

I'm not sure if everyone feels this way after a crisis of that magnitude, but for me, the more I talked about the *Costa Concordia* disaster, the more I realized the severity of what had happened to us. It was therapeutic for me, especially in those early days, being able to let it all out in the several interviews that we did during our first few weeks at home. I'm sure it helped that everyone we dealt with was incredibly understanding of our needs, but the whole experience of telling our story went a long way in helping me to realize that there would be a long journey ahead to get past that terrible night.

Costa began harassing us with phone calls and letters within a day or two of our homecoming. It was such a drastic change from the total lack of contact they wanted to have with us while we were still at their mercy in Italy. Once we were home, they wanted to spin things to make them look as favorable as possible to the public. Yet in those days right after the wreck, they seemed very disinterested in whether we ate, had clean clothes, got to our embassy, or even got home. Now that we finally were home (no thanks to them), all they wanted to do was find out if we were okay and if we would be interested in accepting their discounted cruises and settlement offers.

To me, the entire incident for them boiled down to dollars and cents. It seemed that the cruise line's first priority when we returned home was to get us to sign a settlement offer as quickly as possible. Never did they question or give us time to ascertain what our actual damages were, physically and emotionally. After going through all of this, we soon realized that it takes time to figure out what the true toll of something like that really is. When we arrived home from this nightmare, we were in a state of shock and only wanted to be with our loved ones. The cruise line wanted it their way though, so they made an offer of a discount on the next voyage we booked with them. Following up that insult, Costa finally found itself forced to offer a payment of just slightly above the standard minimum damages laid out in international and Italian law, which states that once you abandon a ship for any reason, the passengers have to be paid a set amount of money.

Actually, some critics have questioned whether this compulsory compensation is why the captain waited so long to give the abandon-ship signal after he knew the ship was going down. Once that signal was given, the cruise line would have been out a hefty chunk of change for the three thousand passengers that were on the ship. (Only the passengers receive a payout; the one thousand or so crew members aren't included in the compensation requirement.) I truly believe that is why there was such a delay in giving the command to abandon ship.

According to the cruise line, they arrived at their offer by meeting with consumer groups to figure out what the most appropriate offer would be, never letting the public know that the payment was based on existing law. They wanted to take credit themselves for making what they thought was a generous payment offer. The cruise line did not take into consideration at all what anyone's *true* damages were. I'm sure quite a few people lost significantly more than fourteen thousand dollars' worth of property in belongings that had to be left behind in their cabins. One good-sized diamond ring alone could easily be worth more than that—and people tend to take expensive jewelry on cruises (at least as far as I have noticed on all the cruises I've been on before). And that doesn't take into account the mental and emotional scarring that comes from fighting for your life when you're supposed to be on a luxurious vacation.

Costa has always refused to comment on the delay in abandoning the ship, other than generally pointing the finger at the captain. I don't know whether the potential financial loss was a consideration or not, but my guess is that it was. I suspect it also played a factor in Carnival's decision not to evacuate the *Triumph* in early 2013, even when it became a floating cesspool in the Caribbean. I'm sure they would deny that, and I've heard that Carnival listed choppy seas as the main reason they didn't abandon ship in that case, but I find it hard to believe that the financial loss didn't play into their thinking. These are corporations and their main concern is to make money.

As a former navy guy myself, I completely understand now what the great war hero Admiral Dewey meant when he said that he'd rather "go around the world in a well-equipped man-of-war than make a trip across the North Atlantic in a transatlantic vessel." According to him, "[t]he greed for money-making is so great that it is with the sincerest regret that I observe that human lives are never taken into consideration." I can't help but agree with him.

I spent time in the navy during Vietnam, and I can remember six-week periods at sea when we didn't see land. Once we got into port though, we were there for several days to a week, usually. But cruise ships are rarely in port longer than the time needed to unload and reload passengers and supplies. The navy isn't motivated by dollars and cents to keep their ships out to sea though. It makes more sense for the military to keep their ships in working order, even if it means spending a little more time in port or dry dock. But it all comes down to economics with the cruise companies.

THE CAPTAIN CLAIMED HE WAS THROWN OFF THE SHIP AND "LANDED" IN A LIFEBOAT, BUT THERE ARE CLEAR AUDIO RECORDINGS OF THE ITALIAN COAST GUARD ORDERING HIM TO GET BACK ON THE SHIP AND HIM REFUSING TO GO. APPARENTLY HIS ATTITUDE TRICKLED DOWN TO THE OTHER OFFICERS BECAUSE I CAN'T REMEMBER A SINGLE OFFICER WHO STEPPED UP AND STAYED TO DO THE RIGHT THING AND HELP THE PASSENGERS.

Obviously, cruise lines are required to have their ships checked out on a regular basis, but there is no incentive for them to spend any extra time double-checking anything. Most cruise ships aren't registered in the United States either, which means they are governed by the laws of whatever country they are registered in, so far as maintenance regulations are concerned. Even Carnival Cruises, the parent company of Costa, has all but a handful of its ships registered in other countries in order to avoid the labor and taxation laws of the United States. Yet Carnival is considered an American-based company.

Luckily, any country where a cruise ship docks has the right to inspect the vessel, and I'm sure many do, but it still feels like it isn't enough. The International Maritime Organization (IMO), a United Nations body, drafts the regulations that govern cruise lines. But the United Nations has no enforcement powers, so these countries of registration carry the burden of enforcing the regulations, and some are probably more laidback than others. There is no consistency in safety standards for all cruise ships and penalties vary from country to country. One would hope that the need to appear safe to potential passengers would be sufficient to keep cruise lines on their toes when it comes to ship safety, but the recent rash of cruising accidents doesn't seem to back up this theory.

What was equally bothersome to me was the total lack of leadership by the captain and the officers on the ship. The captain claimed he was thrown off the ship and "landed" in a lifeboat, but there are clear audio recordings of the Italian Coast Guard ordering him to get back on the ship and him refusing to go. Apparently his attitude trickled down to the other officers because I can't remember a single officer who stepped up and stayed to do the right thing and help the passengers. I later learned that quite a few of them got off the ship when the captain did.

I do know that the average worker on a cruise ship doesn't get paid very much at all. So I understand the crew members not being willing to risk their lives to save passengers, but the officers and the captain had a duty to protect the passengers—a duty they didn't seem to take too seriously. This lack of concern for their duty may cost several of them jail time.

As to the cruising industry as a whole, it seems to function like any other big business and make its decisions based solely on the bottom line—profits. A portion of those profits goes to paying for the political campaigns of Democrats and Republicans alike in Congress. They also pay lobbyists to actively fight for them any time a bill comes up that may threaten their profits. Short of totally boycotting cruises, I'm not sure what will actually hit home with these companies and force them to make the necessary (and sometimes costly) changes to ensure passenger safety above all else. It worries me though that, despite all the cruising disasters that have occurred recently, people still don't realize the risks they take in stepping on a cruise ship. I hope that our story can at least make people more aware of the possible dangers so that they are better prepared in the event that something else goes wrong on another passenger cruise liner.

PART THREE:

HOW YOU CAN SURVIVE

THIRTY-SIX

THE CRUISING INDUSTRY: PAST, PRESENT, AND FUTURE

In the time that has passed since our family's experience on the *Costa Concordia*, a lot has happened in the cruising industry— several other tragedies have occurred on cruise ships and a few positive changes have been made. Much more needs to be accomplished though. Our hope in telling our story is twofold. First, we hope that the cruising industry will finally take the difficult steps necessary to ensure that cruises are as safe as humanly possible. If

THIRTY-TWO PEOPLE DID NOT WALK AWAY FROM THE *COSTA CONCORDIA* AS WE DID. WE OWE IT TO THEIR MEMORY TO DO WHATEVER NEEDS TO BE DONE TO MAKE SURE THEIR DEATHS WERE NOT IN VAIN AND THAT MORE DEATHS ARE PREVENTED.

they refuse to do so, we hope that the governments around the world do everything in their power to require them to make those changes to improve passenger safety. Second, and most importantly, we hope that you and your family can take something away from our recounting of the time we spent on the *Costa Concordia* and in Italy, so that if you ever find yourself in a similar situation, you will have a frame of reference of what we did to survive. Thirty-two people did not walk away from the *Costa Concordia* as we did. We owe it to their memory to do whatever needs to be done to make sure their deaths were not in vain and that more deaths are prevented. We also owe it to the survivors that are still struggling to get back to their daily lives after living through this nightmare.

THERE WERE PEOPLE ON THE *COSTA CONCORDIA* THAT HAD NEVER BEEN ON A CRUISE BEFORE. THEY GOT ON THAT SHIP READY FOR THE VACATION OF A LIFETIME. THEY NEVER MADE IT OFF ALIVE.

Many people view cruising as a wonderful way to travel and relax and see places all over the world without having to change hotels frequently or fly into multiple airports. Cruising is supposed to be a vacation of convenience as well as a fun and amazing experience. It was convenient, fun, and amazing for our family for many years, until January 13, 2012. No amount of convenience or enjoyable cruising experiences before that day can make up for what we went through fighting for our lives on the ship that night. There were people on the *Costa Concordia* that had never been on a cruise before. They got on that ship ready for the vacation of a lifetime. They never made it off alive. Our point is that it doesn't matter if *most* cruises are safe and incident-free; all it takes is one cruise that *isn't* to change your whole life; or end it.

After the *Costa Concordia* tragedy, several other cruises have captured the attention of the nation when disasters struck them as well. The most notable of these occurred in February of 2013 on board the Carnival ship, the *Triumph*. The ship caught fire off the coast of Mexico and was left without electricity or functional plumbing. It took five long days to get the ship into the port of Mobile, Alabama. The over four thousand people on board were forced to pass those five days in relative darkness, sitting on the decks, playing cards to pass the time, with backed-up toilets and filth literally floating all around them in the hallways. They were eventually given buckets to use as restrooms. It was deplorable.

Passengers of the *Triumph* gave mixed reviews of the crew and the cruise line, some claiming the crew was professional and worked hard to keep things as positive as possible, while others were less forgiving and recounted being lied to about the true status of the situation. Because they weren't evacuated, there was no minimum settlement amount that the cruise line was required to pay out. Instead, Carnival offered each passenger five hundred dollars, full compensation for the cruise, and a free flight back home once they docked in Alabama. Multiple lawsuits are pending in regard to the *Triumph* incident.

One month later, another Carnival ship, the *Dream*, had similar electrical- and plumbing-related issues. Thankfully the ship was in port at St. Maarten and the cruise line sent the passengers home from the island by plane, rather than subjecting them to the lack of power and plumbing on board the ship. Reports were conflicting as to just how long the outages continued, but they were apparently caused by an issue with the diesel generator.

Two more Carnival ships, the *Elation* and the *Legend*, also had minor issues in March of 2013. Additionally, and as if to make matters worse, Carnival faced problems from two of its subsidiary companies, Costa and Princess Cruises, in the year and a half following the *Concordia* tragedy. The *Costa Allegra* was set adrift in the pirate-filled waters of the Indian Ocean only six short weeks after we escaped the shipwreck of the *Concordia*. A fire in the generator knocked out power to the ship, and a fishing vessel had to tow it to safety at a nearby island. Then in April of 2013, the *Crown Princess* had a blockage in its vacuum toilet system, leaving more than four hundred staterooms without functioning toilets for over twelve hours.

Carnival and its subsidiary Costa Cruises are facing multiple lawsuits stemming from the *Concordia* and these other disasters. As with most extensive civil suits, they will probably drag out for years. In the meantime, the captain of the *Costa Concordia*, Francesco Schettino, and several other officers are still involved in lengthy criminal proceedings regarding their actions on board the ship and their untimely departure from it. At the time we are writing this, all criminal proceedings are still in progress. Meanwhile, the company itself, Costa Cruises, took a plea bargain and paid a fine of 1.3 million dollars, rather than taking its chances in a criminal trial.

The Carnival Corporation, parent company of Costa, also has multiple other subsidiary cruise lines under its wing, including the Cunard line in the United Kingdom, Princess Cruises, P&O Cruises in both the United Kingdom and Australia, AIDA Cruises in Germany, and several others. Carnival is based out of Miami, Florida, but very few of its ships are actually registered in the United States. Most are registered in the Bahamas and Panama, enabling the company to avoid both U.S. tax laws and U.S. labor laws. It's important to understand that most employees of cruise ships work for a fraction of our minimum wage. Knowing how little most of them earn helped to make us more understanding when the crew of the *Costa Concordia* wasn't always extremely helpful. When you combine poor pay and bad training, it's to be expected that the crew members are either unwilling or unprepared (or both) to risk their lives for the passengers.

The cruising industry isn't without some very necessary and useful safety regulations. Thanks in large part to the aftermath of the *Titanic*, there are laws and guidelines in place in most developed coastal countries, as well as internationally, that are there to protect the lives of the passengers and crew. Cruise ships and their parent companies are governed by various laws in the countries in which they dock and the countries in which they are registered, as well as the International Maritime Organization's International Safety Management Code and the International Convention of the Safety of Life at Sea (SOLAS). Additionally, the Cruise Lines International Association, Inc. (CLIA) has put forth some of its own regulations, the most recent one being the adoption of the "Cruise Industry Passenger Bill of Rights." The bill was originally proposed by Senator Charles Schumer of New York. Senator Jay Rockefeller of West Virginia has also been proactive in attempting to make cruising safer for people in the United States. We're sure that Senator Smith, the man behind the changes brought about after the *Titanic* went down in 1912, would be proud of these two senators for the work they have done one hundred years later.

But there is so much more to do. The Passenger Bill of Rights is a step in the right direction. We've included the Bill of Rights for you on page 235. CLIA also keeps it posted on their website, www. cruising.org. Anyone considering taking a cruise should become familiar with it. We believe though, as a family who endured a horrible experience on a cruise, that there are other steps the cruising industry could take in order to make passengers feel safer.

For example, an international overhaul of the rights of crew members is needed so that the individuals who work on these ships are paid better and trained better. We met so many crew members that night who were just as scared as we were and equally unsure of what to do in that situation. Because of the way cruise ships are registered, there is little or no regulation of crew members' wages. It will take the cruise lines themselves stepping up and doing the right thing before anything is changed.

We also feel that the Bill of Rights did not go nearly as far as it could have towards bringing about change. Several of the "rights" on the list were already in place on almost all cruise ships—despite the lack of a set code—such as adequate medical attention and the right to disembark at a dock, barring dangerous situations on land. (See our full responses to each right on page 237.) The idea of codifying these rights is a great one because it sets down definitively what the cruise lines have to abide by in *all* cases. But we would have liked to see a few more specific rights. For example, the passengers on board the *Triumph* were stuck at sea for five days without adequate plumbing or power, yet the ship was not evacuated. Perhaps it was due to weather, or perhaps it was because the cruise line would have had to pay out to every passenger if they had given the abandon-ship signal. Either way, a more structured "right" to be taken off the ship, should conditions get to that point, needs to be considered.

We understand that no corporation is perfect and that everything in life has risks. However, if the airlines were allowed to run in the same manner that the cruise lines do, the nation would be in an uproar. Senator Smith wondered at the same thing during the *Titanic* hearings when he considered the way the shipping industry ran compared to the railroads. Airlines based in the U.S. could never dodge U.S. laws by registering their planes in other countries to which they occasionally fly. Yet American cruise lines routinely do this with their ships. It is the key elements of cruising, such as this, that need further inspection, both by the government and by the cruise lines themselves.

Change is slow. Our family (and most of our friends who are close enough to know our story intimately) will not step foot on board another cruise ship until we see some serious change. Right now, all we've seen is tragedy after tragedy, some minor, some much greater. But we understand the lure of cruising, probably more than most people, because it was such an intricate part of our family for so long. We want others to be as safe as possible when they cruise (if they choose to do so) and in general when they travel, especially internationally. So we've compiled some of the things we've learned, both over the years and from our time on board the *Costa Concordia* and in Italy, as we struggled to find our way back home.

It is our greatest wish that you and your family can enjoy traveling and be as safe as possible until the cruising industry takes the necessary steps to ensure that every passenger on every ship is free to enjoy a cruising vacation, without being nagged by "what ifs" and worried about what could go wrong. Until that day arrives, we hope these travel tips will help you if you ever find yourself in a situation where there is an emergency on a cruise ship.

We are a living example of what you can do to survive. We did things that we never thought we were capable of doing. If you ever do find yourself in a situation like we did, it is our hope that our story will serve as a reminder that you can survive and overcome any obstacles that you come up against. You must have confidence in yourself and reach down and pull up all your strength and stamina and stay the course to make it through such serious circumstances. But we know you can do it because we did it. We wish you happy, healthy, and safe travels in your journeys, wherever they may take you!

INTERNATIONAL CRUISE LINE
PASSENGER BILL OF RIGHTS

The Members of the Cruise Lines International Association are dedicated to the comfort and care of all passengers on oceangoing cruises throughout the world. To fulfill this commitment, our Members have agreed to adopt the following set of passenger rights:

1. The right to disembark a docked ship if essential provisions such as food, water, restroom facilities, and access to medical care cannot adequately be provided onboard, subject only to the Master's concern for passenger safety and security and customs and immigration requirements of the port.

2. The right to a full refund for a trip that is canceled due to mechanical failures, or a partial refund for voyages that are terminated early due to those failures.

3. The right to have available on board ships operating beyond rivers or coastal waters full-time, professional emergency medical attention, as needed until shore side medical care becomes available.

4. The right to timely information updates as to any adjustments in the itinerary of the ship in the event of a mechanical failure or emergency, as well as timely updates of the status of efforts to address mechanical failures.

S.0.S

5. The right to a ship crew that is properly trained in emergency and evacuation procedures.

6. The right to an emergency power source in the case of a main generator failure.

7. The right to transportation to the ship's scheduled port of disembarkation or the passenger's home city in the event a cruise is terminated early due to mechanical failures.

8. The right to lodging if disembarkation and an overnight stay in an unscheduled port are required when a cruise is terminated early due to mechanical failures.

9. The right to have included on each cruise line's website a toll-free phone line that can be used for questions or information concerning any aspect of shipboard operations.

10. The right to have this *Cruise Line Passenger Bill of Rights* published on each line's website.

OUR RESPONSE TO THE INTERNATIONAL CRUISE LINE PASSENGER BILL OF RIGHTS

1.   In our travel experiences, we have always had the right to get off a docked ship, for any reason, as long as the country in which we were disembarking accepted us. In fact, in the second cruise that we had planned for right after the *Costa Concordia,* we were going to disembark from the cruise in Athens, Greece, instead of completing the cruise back to Italy.

2.   This right only allows you a refund if it is due to mechanical failures. What about human error like on the *Costa Concordia* or injury due to illnesses contracted on board a cruise?

3.   The cruise lines already have emergency medical personnel. Most cruises have a full-time doctor and nurses.

4.   Who will disseminate this information?

5.   Staff and crew are trained, but they need cross-training so that, in case of an emergency, the personnel will know how to perform multiple tasks in the event that the people responsible are unable to function in their capacity.

6.   The ships already have back-up systems so this is not anything new.

7.   This needs to be expanded to include not just mechanical failures but emergency due to human error and infectious diseases.

8. This too needs to be expanded to include things beyond mechanical failures.

9. They already have a toll-free number. They need to have staff that can handle and inform people of accurate information. Debbie called a toll-free number for the *Costa Concordia* disaster and they weren't able to assist her at all. In fact, they were rude to her more than once when she called them.

10. The Passenger Bill of Rights should be posted in every state room and on every travel contract by every cruise line.

THIRTY-SEVEN

WHAT YOU NEED TO KNOW: A LIST OF TIPS, INFO, AND STRATEGIES TO TAKE WITH YOU ON YOUR NEXT VACATION

PRE-PLANNING TRAVEL

Buy Travel Insurance

Most people travel with at least a few expensive items, whether it's their jewelry, their luggage, or their tech gear, not to mention their clothes and wallets. On a trip, anything can happen. Everything we took on the *Costa Concordia*, except the clothes we had on our back and Dean's wallet and BlackBerry, wound up in the Mediterranean Sea. But other things can happen even on dry land. Tourists are easy prey for muggings, hotel rooms and staterooms get broken into, and airlines lose luggage. Be careful though—travel insurance does protect some of your things but not all. Be sure you read the detailed policy carefully, as they have limitations on what they will pay out for computers and personal items and several other things. Don't count on them covering everything you lost. Some policies also cover anything from standard medical expenses to accidental death to trip cancellation refunds. It is a must-have for any trip, but shop carefully for a plan that will fit your needs.

Make Sure the People at Home Are Well-Informed

Even if you're not traveling out of the country, make sure someone at home knows where you're going, the routes and carriers you'll be on, and a general time frame of where you'll be and when. If you're going on a cruise, leave a copy of the cruise ship's itinerary with them so they know what ports you'll be at and when you'll be there. Be sure to leave them the contact information for the ship, as well as a copy of your passport, so they will be able to reach you in case of an emergency.

A Word from Debbie

If your travel takes you out of the country, make sure at least one of your closest relatives at home has a current valid passport. I can't tell you how sick I felt when I realized I might not be able to get to my family in Italy if they needed me! It's a horrible feeling. If you're the one staying behind while your loved ones go abroad, that doesn't mean you don't need to update your passport as well. If disaster strikes overseas, you don't want to be at home worrying about getting an emergency passport when time is of the essence. You want to be able to get to your family as quickly as possible!

And Speaking of Passports

Always make a copy of your passport that you can keep on you at all times when you're out of the country. You can even scan a copy and email it to yourself so that you can access it from your phone (assuming your phone has email capabilities). You could also take a picture with your phone. A paper copy is still probably the safest backup though, just in case something happens to your phone. Remember to keep it on you at all times, that way you can at least prove who you are, even if the original is lost or stolen.

Don't Forget the Medications

If you or a family member takes any type of prescription medications, try to get extra refills to take with you and make sure to get a paper copy of the prescription as well. It's also a good idea to leave a list of all prescriptions, and a copy of the prescriptions themselves, with someone who won't be with you on the trip, as well as the contact information for the prescribing doctor. That way you have a backup in case the need arises for an emergency refill when you're abroad. Also, if your medications are vital to your health, carry them on you at all times. It may not be a bad idea to have a medical alert bracelet if your condition warrants it.

Call Your Cell Phone Carrier

Most people don't like to pay for an international cell phone plan if they don't have to, but we recommend that you call your service provider and ask if they at least offer an emergency international plan. Don't forget to check and see if there is service available at your destination.

Register Online with the State Department Before You Leave
- -

The U.S. Department of State allows you to register online before you travel abroad. Entering your information before you leave allows them to better assist you in the case of an emergency while you're out of the country.

Familiarize Yourself with Your Embassy Before You Leave
- -

We had no idea that some embassies have hours of operation, but when we called the U.S. embassy in Rome for assistance, we were told to get there by a certain time. If you're traveling abroad, look up the information on the embassy nearest to where you'll be and become familiar with their protocol and their hours. It's possible that some embassies will send someone to help you, but the one in Rome required that we come to them. Know as much as you can before you visit a foreign country.

Look at the Tickets Before You Buy Them
- -

Cruise tickets are contracts, and once you purchase them, you're basically stuck with the terms of that contract. The only way to avoid the terms you don't like is to lose the money you spent and not take the cruise, unless you have a travel insurance policy that will cover an early cancellation. If you can, try to get a copy of the ticket contract before you buy the tickets, and familiarize yourself with the terms of the contract so that you are at least aware of what rights you have and don't have.

GENERAL TRAVEL TIPS

Trust Your Instincts

When traveling anywhere, remember to trust your instincts—that voice in your head or bad feeling you have may be your best line of defense if you find yourself in a questionable or dangerous situation abroad. If something doesn't feel right to you, there's a good chance it probably isn't. We were originally told that there was only an "electrical problem" on the ship, but we all knew deep down that it had to be more than that—and we were right.

Use Common Sense

It may seem obvious, but always use common sense when making decisions while you're traveling. It's easy to fall into the trap of just following directions when you're on a tour or a cruise or anything else that has a leader giving instructions. But just because you're being told to do something, doesn't mean it's the smartest thing to do. We aren't advocating mutiny by any means, but just make sure you think through the directions you're given. If they don't make good, common sense, you might want to dig a little deeper before following along blindly.

A Word from Valerie

While I've always considered myself a positive person, I'm also somewhat of a "worrier" because I tend to anticipate bad things that can happen in a tense situation. When we were on the *Costa Concordia*, that tendency to think the worst became my greatest asset. I could think through the bad "what ifs" that many people wanted to ignore and consider what our best course of action would be if the worst were to actually happen. When you're on vacation, the last thing you want to think about is a tragedy happening—problems with the plane, a bad wreck, illness, a mugging, or a shipwreck. But if you think through all the different scenarios that *could* happen and decide what you would do if they *did* happen, you'll be that much more prepared if, God forbid, you find yourself in one of those situations.

BE A SMART CRUISER

A Word from Cindy

For much of the time that we were on the *Costa Concordia*, we were surrounded by panic. Yet panicking and overreacting are two of the worst things you can do in a disaster. Not only was it very frustrating for me to watch, but it didn't help matters at all. In fact, it made things worse. When someone panics, it starts a chain reaction that is very difficult to reel back in. People don't think straight when they're in a panic. So don't add to an already difficult ordeal by becoming dramatic. Be calm and think about what you should do in your situation. And if you see people around you who are panicking, try to calm them down, if possible. It goes back to what Val said—if you've already considered the worst that could happen to you while on vacation, you have no reason to panic if it actually does.

Never Separate from Your Travel Companions

- -

The people you are traveling with are your best allies in a tragedy. They know you and you know them, and chances are they'll be more likely to help you than anyone else, and vice versa. If you're very close, you probably each know how the other thinks, so you have a greater ability to comfort each other when times are difficult. We know that occasionally you will want to do things on your own on a trip, but if you have to split up, make sure the others in your group know where you'll be and when you'll be returning. If at all possible though, at least stay in pairs. Remember, there is safety in numbers.

Watch Your Alcohol Intake

- -

It was difficult enough to maneuver on a sideways ship when we were sober, but I can't imagine doing so if we had been even a little bit under the influence. Many people think of vacation as a time to cut loose and, for some people, that involves heavy drinking. But it can be very dangerous to have too many drinks when you're traveling. Not only are you not at your best (either mentally or physically), but you don't always know the laws of the country you're in (or the laws governing the ship you're on). It's very easy to find yourself on the wrong side of the drinking laws in a country where you may not even speak the language. So for safety's sake, keep the drinking to a minimum so that you have all your wits about you if you need them.

Keep Money on You at All Times

It's easy to run down to the hotel bar without your wallet if you know you can charge things to your room, or go to dinner on a cruise ship without grabbing your purse. But as tempting as it sounds to not have to keep up with a wallet or purse, having cash or a credit card on you at all times can make a huge difference if you find yourself in a situation like we did. We were extremely lucky that Dean had his wallet. We wouldn't have even been able to get coffee and a snack at that café on Giglio if Dean hadn't kept his wallet in his pocket, let alone pay for a cab to get to the embassy in Rome. You never know when you'll need emergency funds, so keep them on you, even if you have to get a money belt or have a small pocket sewn into the lining of a jacket.

A Word from Georgia

If I hadn't unpacked when we got to our cabin, I might not have known where those three life jackets were when we so desperately needed them. When you first get on the ship, find out where the life jackets are kept. Familiarize yourself with your cabin and where the life jackets are in the room, and ask or look around to discover where others are kept around the ship. Be aware that there are usually life jackets on the lifeboats as well. If the crew would have given us some life jackets from one of the lifeboats, we would not have had to take the risk we took in going back to our cabin.

Get to Know the Lay of the Land

Once you know where the life jackets are, find out where everything else is. Where are the stairs nearest to your cabin? Where is your muster station? What is the quickest way to your muster station? Is there a back way in case of a fire or crowds? Also, familiarize yourself with other muster stations. If you are far away from your own during a tragedy, you can always go to the nearest one, so find the closest muster station to all the places you plan on visiting, such as the pools, restaurants, bars, and casinos. It's your responsibility to know your way around the ship—don't expect the crew to come find you if a tragedy does occur. Plan ahead!

Be Cautious

Remember that a cruise ship is like a small floating city, filled with many different types of people. Most are great individuals, but as in any town, there are always people who won't think twice about hurting you or stealing from you. Just because you're on vacation doesn't mean you can let your guard down around strangers. No matter how much you think you've gotten to know someone in a few days on a ship, remember, they're still strangers and you need to use caution in what you tell them and how much you trust them.

IN THE EVENT OF A DISASTER ON ON A CRUISE SHIP

Be Proactive If You Are the Victim of a Crime

The laws that apply on cruise ships can be murky. If the ship is at port, the law of that country applies; if the ship is not in territorial water, maritime law applies. This can make for some confusion for the crew if you report a crime to them, so always make sure to follow up and make certain that the proper authorities were contacted. Again, don't expect others to help you—stand up for yourself and make sure the correct actions are taken immediately.

Never Go Into "Crew Only" Areas

Even if a crew member invites you into a restricted area, politely decline. Having passengers in these "crew only" areas can be dangerous. Stay in the areas designated for passengers.

Choose Sensible Footwear

We were fortunate in that we all had on sensible shoes. Many women on the *Costa Concordia* weren't so lucky though. They had been wearing heels to dinner, and when the ship started listing, they had to abandon their shoes and go barefoot in wet, chilly weather. While it may be tempting to strap on the stilettos for the fancy dinners, be aware that if you find yourself in a situation like we did, you may wind up in bare feet (and could easily cut your foot) or risk twisting or breaking an ankle. Many survivors on board the *Costa Concordia* suffered from injuries to their feet since they had to get rid of their heels in order to try to stay balanced.

Don't Disembark Alone

Again, we can't stress how important it is to stay with people you know when you're traveling, and that's especially true when you get off at ports. If you decide to go ashore at any or all of the stops that the ship makes, be sure to go with at least one of your traveling companions and stay with them while you're on land.

Be Germ-Conscious

There have been multiple cases of people contracting contagious diseases while on cruise ships. For that reason, ships routinely have sanitizer machines and hand wipes in restaurants and scattered in various locations around the ship. Take full advantage of them. Cruise ships may be large, but they are still a confined space filled with people that you don't know. Be vigilant with hand-washing. It may not be a bad idea to carry a small bottle of hand sanitizer with you as well.

Never Climb on Railings

There have been cases of people falling overboard on cruise ships. While it may be tempting to reenact the scene from the

Titanic movie, you're much safer to steer clear of the railings. If you're traveling with children, make sure to keep them away from the railings as well, and resist the temptation to set them on the railings so that they can see out.

Avoid Elevators

Just like you wouldn't take the elevators in a building if there were a fire or a bomb threat, don't be tempted to take them if something goes wrong on a cruise ship. Stick with the stairs—they're much safer.

Know the Emergency Signal

The emergency signal on a ship is seven short blasts followed by one long blast. Find a recording of the signal before you ever step foot on a cruise ship and listen to it several times so that you are very familiar with it. You should also listen carefully to this signal when they sound it during a muster drill. In the event that the PA system isn't working or that you don't speak the primary language on the ship, knowing the emergency signal when you hear it can make a difference by giving you valuable extra minutes that other people may not have if they're standing around wondering what that noise is.

Stay on Deck

While we admit that we went back to our stateroom to get

life jackets, we made that decision out of necessity. It can be very dangerous to leave the decks during an emergency. On the *Costa Concordia*, some crew members actually told people to return to their staterooms in the midst of the disaster. Remember, even if you're told to return to your cabin, if the ship is clearly in trouble and you think an evacuation is imminent, stay on deck. This is one of those times that common sense and instinct should take precedence over what you have been told. Pay close attention to the situation before you go blindly back to your cabin during an emergency.

Activate Your Life Jacket Lights

The lights on a life jacket are designed to come on once they hit water, but if you find yourself in the dark and still on the ship, or even in a lifeboat, you can activate the lights by using your own saliva. It's definitely better than being stuck in the dark! We utilized that technique when we tried to get the helicopters flying above to rescue us. Even though they didn't attempt a rescue, we felt that we were doing our part to make them aware that we needed help.

Don't Blindly Rely on Evacuation Protocol

Just because we have the general rule of "women and children first" doesn't mean everyone follows it. Unfortunately, we were shocked to see that many men did not follow that rule on the *Costa Concordia*. There were gentlemen that allowed some women and children to go in front of them onto a lifeboat, but don't stand by meekly waiting for that to happen. Be assertive, especially if you are traveling with children, so that you can guarantee that you will get them a spot in a lifeboat.

Keep to High Ground

If you find yourself in a situation like we did on the *Costa Concordia*, unable to get or stay on a lifeboat, make your way to the highest point of the ship. The scene in the movie *Titanic* where Jack and Rose climb to the highest part of the ship and hang on until the very end actually happened to one man. Archibald Gracie survived the sinking of the *Titanic* by doing exactly what Jack and Rose did—he climbed up to the highest rail and rode the ship down until it hit the water and he could kick his way to the surface. Hopefully you'll be rescued long before it comes to that, but keep to high ground whenever possible.

Jump in the Water as an ABSOLUTE Last Resort

More people died from exposure in the cold North Atlantic waters than drowned when the *Titanic* sank. Even in the Mediterranean Sea, where we were, the waters were still very cold. Hypothermia sets in quickly in the water. You can't guarantee that you'll be picked up by a lifeboat or be able to make it to shore, no matter how close it seems to be, so only jump in if you have no other choices available. Even in warmer waters, there are other considerations, such as choppy seas and dangerous fish.

A Word from Dean

During my time in the navy, I was trained on the proper way to jump into the water wearing a life jacket, and I've made sure to educate my wife and daughters on this as well. Just because you're wearing a life jacket does not mean you can jump off the side of the ship and safely land in the water. Life jackets are meant to keep you afloat, not cushion your fall. If you can, take a water safety course on how to properly wear and use a life jacket before you ever go on a cruise.

Finally, From All of Us

Our family has always loved to travel because it allowed us to explore the world together. If we can leave you with one final tip, it would be that you enjoy your travels and form great memories from them, as we have. Despite all that we lost on the Costa Concordia, no one can ever take those other happy memories away from us. We encourage you to travel safely and make some happy memories of your own!

BIBLIOGRAPHY

Bone, James. "Probe Into Costa Concordia's Abandon Ship Delay." *Australian*, January 20, 2012. Reprinted from *Times*. http://www.theaustralian.com.au/news/world/probe-into-costa-concordias-abandon-ship-delay/story-e6frg6so-1226249259312.

Brown, Genevieve Shaw. "Second Carnival Cruise Ship Having Trouble at Sea." *ABC News*, March 15, 2013. http://abcnews.go.com/Travel/carnival-cruise-ship-trouble-sea/story?id=18735104#.UbETLb7n8ic.

Carnival Corporation & PLC. http://phx.corporate-ir.net/phoenix.zhtml?c=140690&p=irol-index.

"Carnival Elation Gets Precautionary Tug Escort After 'Minor Issue.'" *WDSU News*, March 10, 2013. http://www.wdsu.com/news/local-news/new-orleans/Carnival-Elation-gets-precautionary-tug-escort-after-minor-issue/-/9853400/19257884/-/82ckl2z/-/index.html.

"Costa Concordia: What Happened." *BBC News: Europe*, July 9, 2013. http://www.bbc.co.uk/news/world-europe-16563562.

"Cruise Industry Adopts Passenger Bill of Rights." *CLIA*, May 22, 2013. http://www.cruising.org/news/press_releases/2013/05/cruise-industry-adopts-passenger-bill-rights.

"Cruise to Disaster." First broadcast July 4, 2012 by CNN.

"Despite Compensation Offer, Italian Cruise Ship Survivors Sue for Damages." *CNN*, January 27, 2012. http://www.cnn.com/2012/01/27/world/europe/italy-cruise-ship.

Fitzpatrick, Judy. "Carnival Dream Cruise Ship Reports Problems in St. Maarten." *Huffington Post*, March 14, 2013. http://www.huffingtonpost.com/2013/03/14/carnival-dream-cruise-ship-trouble_n_2875153.html.

Hetter, Katia. "Cruise Ship Suffers Stopped-up Toilets." *CNN: Travel*, April 15, 2013. http://www.cnn.com/2013/04/15/travel/crown-princess-toilets.

Johanson, Mark. "Are Cruise Ships Safe? Carnival Cruises' Triumphant Fall from Grace Raises the Question of Whether Cruise Vacations are too Risky." *International Business News Times*, April 6, 2013. http://www.ibtimes.com/are-cruise-ships-safe-carnival-cruises-triumphant-fall-grace-raises-question-whether-cruise-1170573#.

Kington, Tom. "Costa Concordia Firm Fined $1.3 Million for Shipwreck off Italy." *Los Angeles Times*, April 10, 2013. http://articles.latimes.com/2013/apr/10/world/la-fg-wn-costa-concordia-fine-20130410.

Mungin, Lateef, and Steve Almasy. "Crippled Cruise Ship Returns; Passengers Happy to be Back." *CNN: Travel*, February 15, 2013. http://www.cnn.com/2013/02/14/travel/cruise-ship-fire/index.html.

"Must a Captain Be the Last One Off a Sinking Ship?" *BBC News Magazine*, January 18, 2012. http://www.bbc.co.uk/news/magazine-16611371.

Nadeau, Barbie Latza. "How Much Are the 'Costa Concordia' Passengers Entitled to Win—and Who Is Accountable for the Shipwreck?" *Daily Beast*, February 8, 2012. http://www.thedailybeast.com/articles/2012/02/08/how-much-are-the-costa-concordia-passengers-entitled-to-win-and-who-is-accountable-for-the-shipwreck.html.

Piore, Adam. "How Safe Is Your Cruise Ship?" *Condé Nast Traveler: The Informer*, June 2012. http://www.cntraveler.com/cruises/2012/06/special-report-cruise-safety-regulations-costa-concordia.

"Stricken Costa Allegra Being Towed to Safety Through Pirate Zone." *NBC News: Travel*, February 28, 2012. http://www.nbcnews.com/travel/stricken-costa-allegra-being-towed-safety-through-pirate-zonestricken-cruise-235344.

Wade, Wyn Craig. *The Titanic: Disaster of a Century*. New York: Skyhorse Publishing, Inc., 2012.

Pisa, Nick. "'Don't Worry, Go Back to Your Cabins, It's Just an Electrical Fault': What Stricken Cruise Ship Passengers Were Told After Hitting Rocks." *Daily Mail: Mail Online*, January 20, 2012. http://www.dailymail.co.uk/news/article-2089339/Costa-Concordia-passengers-told-to-cabins-cruise-ship-hit-rocks.html.

Walker, James. "What Cruise Lines Don't Want You to Know." *CNN: Opinion*, February 14, 2013. http://www.cnn.com/2013/02/13/opinion/walker-cruise-ships.

Winfrey, Oprah. "Winfrey's Commencement Address." *Harvard Gazette*, May 31, 2013. http://news.harvard.edu/gazette/story/2013/05/winfreys-commencement-address/.